Biblical Christmas Performances

Plays, Poems, Choral Readings, Stories and Songs

Compiled by
Rebecca Daniels

illustrated by
Janet Skiles

Cover by Janet Skiles

Shining Star Publications, Copyright © 1988
A Division of Good Apple, Inc.

ISBN No. 0-86653-461-X

Standardized Subject Code TA ac

Printing No. 987654321

Shining Star Publications
A Division of Good Apple, Inc.
Box 299
Carthage, IL 62321-0299

Unless otherwise indicated, the King James Version of the Bible was used in preparing the activities in this book.

TO THE TEACHER/PARENT

Here it is! Everything you will need to stage a Christmas performance that will dazzle everyone—have them standing in ovation and shouting ENCORE! Whether you are planning an informal 5-minute recitation for a small family group in your kitchen or a 2-hour musical play and song presentation to be delivered to a whole congregation or school, on a stage with costumes and scenery, your performance is guaranteed to be GREAT with the original stories, choral readings, poems, plays and songs found herein.

Begin by reading and recording the titles of selections appropriate for your group. As time allows, share the stories, plays, poems and songs with the children to discover which ones they like best. The performance is bound for success if the children have their hearts and hands in the selection of materials to be presented. Reproduce enough copies of play scripts, choral reading recitations, songs, etc., as needed for your group. Make sure there are plenty of rehearsals so that everything will go smoothly on stage! Costume directions and patterns that can be enlarged for scenery backdrops are included to add that special touch to your Christmas performance. This Christmas present a performance that will live in the hearts of your children forever while entertaining your audience with the true meaning of Christmas!

TABLE OF CONTENTS

Shining Star Publications, Copyright © 1988, A Division of Good Apple, Inc.

SS1868

CHRISTMAS STORIES

Shining Star Publications, Copyright © 1988, A Division of Good Apple, Inc.

454338

SS1868

I LOVE TO TELL THE STORY

Tips for Storytellers

The art of storytelling has been cultivated in all ages among people who have left any records. It is an outcome of instinct that seems to be planted universally in the human mind.

Stories were told by mothers of the wildest tribes as well as those of the more advanced races. Little ones were hushed to sleep by stories. Weary hunters often sat around a fire amusing themselves with curious tales of the hunt.

Children have great imaginations. They can easily imagine that clouds are boats, dogs or mountains according to their shape or size. One child asked the teacher if clouds were angel's clothes. So with such imagination in the minds of an audience the storyteller is right at home.

In earlier years there was usually one person in every community who excelled in the art of storytelling, someone whose imagination and memory was exceptionally good. This person was in great demand and never lacked for listeners.

Today we have so many wonderful books and magazines for children. Anyone can be a good storyteller with a little practice. One does not need to do a story without a book, but should be able to carry on with it by looking at the listeners while reading. The voice should sound as though the teller is speaking, rather than reading.

The following suggestions may help the beginning story-teller to be successful.
1. Be thoroughly familiar with the selection to be interpreted.
2. Learn to create moods, impressions.
3. Read dramatically but naturally.
4. Use gestures, pauses, changes in rate of reading.
5. Develop the ability to keep children as good listeners. If they become restless after a short period of time, present a dramatic pause using facial expression as if to say "Wonder what comes next?"

Children in small groups make a better audience but a good storyteller can hold the attention of a large group. It takes practice, proper projection of voice, perfect enunciation and timing. If this can be accomplished no microphone will be needed. Teach children to listen by the storytelling method. It really works!

After children have enjoyed a story let them dramatize it in their own fashion: pantomime while the story is being read or rewrite the story as a play. Even children in first grade can do this in the simplest form.

Children also enjoy taking an idea from a story and developing their own. The more writing children do the better developed their imaginations will become. The students of today need all the creative writing they can get from first grade on through school.

Only a Grain of Corn

by Anne Evans

Wee Mouse ran back to the stable, a grain of corn grasped firmly in her teeth.

She tucked the corn in her nest. "I have three grains of corn," she said. "I won't starve." How good she felt.

Then one day a great commotion was heard in the barnyard.

"Have you heard?" clucked the hen. "Three kings have come to town. Their camels are in the stable. And each king is carrying a precious gift."

"I never saw a king before," said Wee Mouse. "I wish I could see them."

"See them indeed!" scoffed the hen. "What chance would a poor mouse like you have to see three such wise men? Better you should go to the stable and talk to the camels."

And that is just what Wee Mouse did. She found the camels eating their meal.

"Plenty of food for camels," sighed Wee Mouse, "but never enough for a mouse like me." Then she thought of her three grains of corn and she felt better.

"Oh, great camel," she said, "where are you headed?"

The camel looked down at Wee Mouse though half-closed eyelids. "We are following a star. We are going to Bethlehem."

"To Bethlehem?" asked the mouse.

"Yes, to Bethlehem. A Savior has been born and the kings are bringing Him great and costly gifts."

"A Savior! How I should like to see Him," said Wee Mouse.

"And what would you give Him?" asked the camel. "It's a wonder you manage to stay alive. Look at how thin you are."

"I guess you're right," sighed Wee Mouse, and she went back to her nest.

Suddenly she had an idea!

"I do have a gift for the Savior!" she cried. "I do. I do. I will give Him my three grains of corn. I will follow the star and I will see the Savior."

So she gathered up her three grains of corn and followed the camels and the star. But it was cold on the desert at night and Wee Mouse shivered as she ran along trying to keep up with the camels.

Wee Mouse was tired. Her feet hurt. But still she ran on, clutching her grains of corn.

At last dawn broke and the kings stopped at an inn to rest. Wee Mouse hid in the stable and made a nest for herself. She tucked the three grains of corn in a corner of the nest.

Just then, a big rat came by.

"Oh, ho," said the rat, "I spy some grains of corn. I think I'll have some."

"No, no," cried Wee Mouse. "you can't have any of this corn. It's for the Savior. I've been running all night across the desert just to give it to Him."

But the rat grabbed a grain of corn and ran off.

"Come back! Come back!" cried Wee Mouse. But the rat ran on.

Two great tears ran down Wee Mouse's cheeks. She was very hungry. But she could not go in search of food. She must stay and guard her gift.

Weak with hunger, Wee Mouse made ready for the trip across the desert as soon as the sun had set.

Again the stars twinkled in the heavens. One star shone brighter than the others, guiding the three kings and Wee Mouse to the town of Bethlehem.

On and on Wee Mouse ran, falling often as her legs gave out from under her.

Finally they stopped for a moment and Wee Mouse caught up with them. She leaned against the camel's foot for support.

"Oh, it's you," said the camel as he turned his

head to see what was near his foot. "How did you get here?"

"I've been following you," said Wee Mouse, a sob catching in her throat. "I have a gift for the Savior."

"You . . . a gift for the Savior!" scoffed the camel. "What can you give? Why, my masters are bringing gold and myrrh and frankincense."

Wee Mouse hung her head, almost too ashamed to answer. "I have two grains of corn," she said. "I had three, but a rat stole one of them and now I have only two."

"Grains of corn!" gasped the camel in surprise. "Do you mean to tell me you've run across the desert to give the Savior two grains of corn?"

Wee Mouse thought of her two grains of corn and what they meant to her. "That corn is my treasure," she said. "It means as much to me as all the riches the wise men are bringing to the Savior. Yes, I am going to Bethlehem with my treasure."

The camel could hardly believe it! He looked down at Wee Mouse and suddenly felt sorry for the tiny creature.

"Climb up my leg," he said, "and fasten yourself in the end of my tail, I will carry you to Bethlehem. We should arrive there tomorrow."

So Wee Mouse climbed up the camel's leg and made herself comfortable in the camel's tail. She clutched the two grains of corn to her. Soon she was fast asleep. She slept and slept. She was so tired.

Suddenly, Wee Mouse felt herself being shaken. "Wake up! We're here," cried the camel. And giving his tail a mighty shake he dropped Wee Mouse in the sand. The grains of corn flew in the air.

"My corn! My corn!" shrieked Wee Mouse as she searched through the sand.

"Oh, I'm sorry," said the camel. "I forgot about the corn."

Wee Mouse searched and searched, but only one grain of corn could she find. And taking that last grain, she followed the wise men. "We have come to bring gifts to the Savior," she heard one of them say.

"Come with me," answered a voice, and Wee Mouse followed.

Soon they came to a stable and someone opened a door.

Wee Mouse looked around.

"But it's only a stable," she squeaked. "Just like the one I live in."

Just then, she saw the wise men on their knees offering their gifts to a wee Babe lying in a manger.

Silently, and in awe, the wise men placed their gifts at the feet of the Child.

Wee Mouse felt the grain of corn in her paw. She thought of how hungry she was and how many times she wanted to eat it. She thought of the rat that stole one grain. And she thought of the grain she had lost in the desert. She was ashamed to give the Savior a single grain of corn. Surely there must be a better way to give the Savior what was left of her treasure.

Just then, she heard a wise man say to Joseph, "You must leave now, for a soldier is in town looking for the Savior."

"Yes, we must go," said Joseph, as Mary gathered up the Savior and they fled.

Wee Mouse crept into a corner of the stable clutching her last grain of corn, hoping that the Christ Child would escape.

Soon the soldier entered the stable and tied up his camel while he went into the inn for some food.

Wee Mouse clutched her grain of corn even tighter until it hurt her paw. Just then, the hurt gave her an idea!

Softly, ever so softly, she climbed upon the camel and placed her grain of corn under the camel's saddle. Quietly she crept into a corner and waited.

Then the soldier came out and mounted the camel.

"Whoa!" cried the soldier as the camel started to buck and threw him to the ground. "Whoa!" he cried again and again while the camel continued to buck, the grain of corn pressing firmly into his flesh.

The camel bucked, and the corn pressed, and all the while Mary and Joseph made their escape with the Savior.

It was only a grain of corn, but it was Wee Mouse's gift to the Christ Child—the Savior's escape.

LOVE MAKES A DIFFERENCE

by Sue Hamilton

"Samuel!" shouted Perez, the innkeeper. "Where are you? Come here right now!"

Samuel laid the currycomb on the shelf and hurried from the stable to the inn.

"Where have you been? There are guests coming and we have work to do," said Perez angrily as he boxed Samuel's ears. "Fetch wood for the fires. Fill the water pitchers in the rooms. See that there are fresh pallets in each room. And turn the meat on the spit so it doesn't burn," ordered Perez.

Samuel scurried about doing as Perez had ordered. At last he finished and sat down with a sigh by the fire. Samuel turned the spit slowly. As he crouched over the roast, Samuel began thinking about Perez. "I wonder why Perez is always so angry. I can never seem to please him no matter how hard I try," thought Samuel.

Lost in his daydreams, Samuel didn't hear the guests arriving until Perez gave him a kick, "Go take care of our guests' horses," demanded Perez. Samuel hurried out taking the horses to the stable. There he brushed the horses until their coats gleamed.

Perez doesn't have to be so mean," thought Samuel. "If only he'd say please once in a while." Samuel continued his thinking, "I'd run away, but where could I go? I have no other home."

Quickly he finished grooming the horses, gave them some grain and hay and then hurried back to the inn. There he worked in the kitchen cleaning up after the guests. Samuel was just finishing when he heard Perez at the door say, "But I told you I don't have any more rooms. They are full. You'll have to go elsewhere."

"My wife is going to have a baby," said the man. "Don't you even have a small room we might have, or just the corner of a room?"

"No," stated Perez. "Now go away," As he started to close the door Samuel slipped out. "There is a clean stall in the stable," Samuel informed the man. "I just cleaned it this afternoon. It has fresh hay laid in it. Why don't you come to the stable for the night?"

Samuel led the man and his wife to the stable. As the man helped his wife off the donkey, Samuel saw that they had little bedding. He frowned in thought, then his face lit up. "Wait here," he requested. "I have a warm wool blanket I will get for you."

Samuel hurried to the inn and was back in minutes with his soft wool blanket. He fluffed up the hay and carefully laid the blanket over it. "Who are you?" asked Samuel as he helped the man with his wife.

"My name is Joseph and this is my wife Mary. We came to Bethlehem for the taxation," explained the man.

SS1868

Joseph helped Mary lay down while Samuel led the donkey to a stall and began brushing him. "Have you traveled far?" asked Samuel.

"We have come from Nazareth," replied Joseph. "We have been traveling for two weeks. We came twelve miles today."

"You must be hungry!" exclaimed Samuel. "I'll go to the kitchen and see if there is any roast left."

Samuel quietly crept into the kitchen keeping a look out for Perez. While he peeled the last of the roast from the bone, Samuel remembered the warm blue shawl tucked away in his corner. He ran to get it, then picking up the meat, hurried back to the stable. As he reached the door, Samuel heard a baby cry. Stepping inside, he saw Mary lying on the blanket with the baby beside her. Setting down the roast, Samuel ran over to them. As he knelt in the hay, he gave Mary the shawl. "I brought this for the baby. It was my mother's," explained Samuel. As Mary wrapped the baby in the shawl Samuel asked, "What are you going to name him?"

"His name is Jesus," replied Mary.

Looking at Jesus, Samuel felt all his anger at Perez melt away. What a wonderful thing a baby was! He could feel love stealing into his heart giving him a warm, happy feeling.

Just then they heard Perez at the door of the stable. "What do you want? You can't go in there! Go back where you came from!" shouted Perez angrily.

Looking up, Samuel, Joseph and Mary saw some shepherds crowding into the stable. As the door swung open, the stable was flooded with light from a bright star.

"Where is he? Where is the baby? We have come to see him. The angels told us he would be here. They said he's the Messiah." The shepherds all talked at once. Perez tried to keep them out of the stable, but they just pushed him aside.

Perez followed the shepherds into the stable. He saw one of the shepherds laying a soft white sheep fleece over the baby. Then looking at Jesus a feeling came over him such as he had never had before. The feeling started at his head and slid over him right down to his toes. He felt a peace and love for his friends and neighbors. He looked at Samuel and realized how badly he had been treating him.

Perez walked over to Samuel and put his hand on his shoulder. "Samuel," he said, "I'm sorry for the way I've treated you. Will you forgive me?"

The shepherds insisted on leaving even though Perez asked them to stay. Perez, with his arm around Samuel, walked back to the inn.

In the stable Mary and Joseph smiled down on their baby. They realized he would have the power to change people's lives. God had indeed sent His Son to save the world.

SS1868

LISTENER, MARY'S DONKEY

by Edith E. Cutting

Listener didn't like the noisy crowds. He hoped Joseph could find a nice quiet stall soon.

At the first inn where they stopped, the owner shouted at them. "No, I don't have any room. Move on! Move on! You're blocking the way."

Joseph asked at the next inn, but the owner just shook his head. "Every room is packed," he said.

They turned down a little side street and Joseph asked again.

"No, no," the man grumbled. "Nobody has any rooms."

"But my wife needs rest," Joseph pleaded.

Listener pushed closer. The owner looked at him and at Mary. At last he said, "There's room for your donkey in the stable, but that's all the room I have."

Listener nudged Joseph. Mary leaned toward him and whispered, "Take it, Joseph. With clean straw it will be fine. I'm sure Listener will share with us."

Joseph nodded. The owner led them around to the clean little stable. "It's far better than a crowded inn." Mary said joyously.

Listener stood quietly and flicked his ears in agreement.

Joseph didn't take long to get clean straw and pile it in the empty stall. Then he spread the saddle blanket over it, and Mary lay down to rest.

"Fill the manger, too," she told him.

"It will make a good bed," he agreed.

Listener shook his head. How could anyone sleep in a manger? It was much too short. He walked over to a corner of the stable where he saw another pile of clean straw.

Later that night Listener was awakened by the door opening. The innkeeper's wife came bustling in, and Listener heard her talking with Mary. He dozed off again.

All of a sudden he heard a baby cry. A baby? Listener's eyes jerked open, and he flicked his ears forward. He heard it again.

"Ah, a fine healthy boy!" he heard the other woman say.

Then he heard Mary's soft voice. "My son," she said. "His name shall be Jesus."

"A good name," Listener thought. He want back to sleep.

A little later that night the door was pushed open again. This time Listener heard men's voices. He scrambled to his feet. Were robbers breaking in? His little hooves tapped quickly towards the stall where Mary was. He would kick them if they hurt her!

But no, the men were kneeling. Robbers would not do that. And Mary was sitting by the manger where a tiny baby in swaddling clothes was lying. So that's whose bed it was!

Listener heard one man speak and then another. "The angels told us where we would find the baby."

"While we were watching our sheep, they sang."

"The baby shall be our Saviour."

"And we have seen Him! Glory to God in the highest!"

Their voices became softer as they saw the baby's eyes close. Slowly they backed out of the stable.

When they were gone, Listener went back to his corner. But he didn't sleep again that night. What things he had heard! Things no donkey had heard before!

When the first bird sang the next morning, Listener went tapping over to the stall where Mary lay. Joseph was just lifting the baby from the manger. He laid him in Mary's arms.

"Come, Listener," said Mary. "See your new master. Will you carry us safely back to Nazareth?"

Listener stretched his neck out till his nose almost touched the baby. He flicked his ears forward, and Mary laughed softly as she reached up and patted him.

Joseph turned to Listener and led him out of doors. It was a beautiful morning. Listener jumped and kicked his heels. He felt like trotting all around the city.

Only—he didn't want to be where he could not hear Mary and the baby. He flicked his ears forward and walked quietly back into the stable.

Shining Star Publications, Copyright © 1988, A Division of Good Apple, Inc.

SS1868

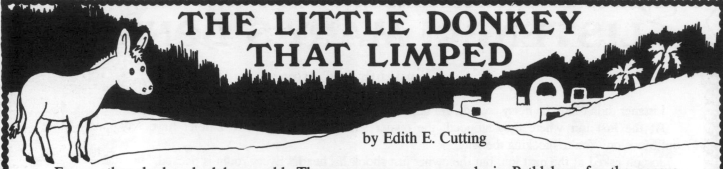

THE LITTLE DONKEY THAT LIMPED

by Edith E. Cutting

Every other donkey had been sold. There were so many people in Bethlehem for the census taking that Lamas could have sold twice as many donkeys if he had had them. One had even been stolen from the backyard of the innkeeper's stable where a man and his wife and baby were staying.

But nobody wanted this little donkey. Lamas kicked at it and turned away. When he had bought the last herd of donkeys, he had not noticed that this one had a stiff leg.

As he latched the gate, a voice behind him asked, "Is that donkey for sale?"

"Yes, if you want him," Lamas grumbled, "but I may as well tell you—he limps."

"Badly?" asked the other man.

"See for yourself," said Lamas. He picked up a stone and threw it. It hit the little donkey, and he started to trot in a jerky way. "The front leg is stiff at the knee," Lamas added. "It is not sore. He's able to walk all right."

The man sighed. "How much do you want for him?" he asked.

They agreed on a price at last, and the man led the little donkey away. When he got to the stable, the woman was waiting with the baby in her arms.

"He's not much good, Mary," said the man. "One leg is stiff, so he limps, but he's all I could find. We must leave at once if we are to get to Egypt safely."

"Oh, Joseph, he's beautiful," she replied, petting the little gray donkey's nose. "I'm sure he will be strong enough to carry the babe and me."

She pulled her blue robe back, and Joseph softly touched the baby's cheek. Then he went to buy food and grain to take with them, and soon they started on their way.

That night they stopped away from the road behind a big rock, where other travelers would not see them and disturb the baby. After they had eaten, Joseph spread the robes for Mary and the baby to sleep on. Then he let the little donkey loose. It would not go far, for he had laid a little hay and grain near them, and there was only barren ground beyond. Then Joseph, too, lay down to sleep.

While it was still dark the next morning, he was awakened by the sound of horses' hooves and squeaking saddle leather. Soldiers, he thought, and turned to make sure Mary kept the baby quiet. He had been warned in a dream that he must leave the country for fear of Herod's soldiers. Had he started too late to save the little one?

Suddenly a rough voice called out, "Here's a stray donkey. There must be people around. Shall we search?"

Joseph heard the uneven tapping of the little donkey's stiff leg, as if he were being driven away.

"Nobody would ride him," another voice answered. "Can't you see he's lame? Let him go. Probably he could not keep up with the herd that went through yesterday. Come along."

The sounds of voices and horses' hooves faded into the distance.

Joseph stood up as the tapping of the litttle donkey's hooves came closer again. He bent down to rub the little gray donkey's stiff leg. "I'm sorry I said you were not much good," he murmured. "You were good enough to save us all from the Roman soldiers."

"Are you sure they are gone?" whispered Mary, holding the baby tightly.

"They are gone," answered Joseph. "They would not stop for our little donkey that limped. His limping has saved us all."

THE SMALL SHEPHERD

by Ellen Javernick

When the angels had gone away into heaven, the shepherds whispered in awed voices to one another. "Let us now go even into Bethlehem," said one tall shepherd. "And see this thing which has come to pass which the Lord hath made known to us."

The tall shepherd was Michael's father. Someday Michael hoped to be strong and tall like his father, but now at seven, Michael was the smallest of the shepherds. Michael had listened in wonder while the angels had told about the baby king born that night. He knew something wonderful was happening. He rolled up the soft blue blanket he used when he sat on the cold ground. "It will be very cold on this wintery night," he thought, "I will take my blanket to the little king when I go to see him in Bethlehem."

Michael felt a hand on his shoulder. He looked up into the weather-roughened face of his father. "You, my son," said the older shepherd, "will stay here to watch our flocks."

"Oh, Father, please let me go with you to see the baby."

"The way is far, my son, and we must make haste. Your legs are short and we would have to go more slowly if you walked with us. We must also think of the sheep. They cannot be left alone. I am sure you will please the baby king if you take good care of the animals while we are away."

"But, Father, I want to go to see the new king."

Michael's words did not change his father's mind and soon the small shepherd was sitting alone in the field looking up at the big star that twinkled brightly in the sky. He pulled the blue blanket over his knees to keep the cold night from making his legs shiver. Suddenly he remembered. The blanket was to have been his present for the little king. "Father, Father," he called, but his father and the other shepherds were too far away to hear him.

His eyes were wet and the tears in them made him blink. He had not been able to go with the others to Bethlehem, and even worse, he had forgotten to send his blanket for the baby's birthday present. The warm, salty tears spilled from his eyes. How he wished he could do something to please the little king, but it didn't seem that there was anything he could do now. Then he remembered what his father had said. He could please the baby by taking good care of the sheep while the other shepherds were away. He rubbed the tears from his face and counted to see if all the sheep were there. While he had been crying he had not been watching the sheep. Maybe one

SS1868

of them had wandered away already. "Thirty-six, thirty-seven," he counted carefully. He could not find the last sheep. The thirty-eighth one was missing. Michael counted again, but he could still find only thirty-seven sheep. His father would never trust him with the animals again, and because he had forgotten his job, he had lost his last chance to please the baby.

I'll have to find the lost sheep, he thought, but where shall I look? Just then he thought he saw something moving in the distance. The dogs helped him gather the other sheep together, and they headed in the direction of the movement. It was slow going, and whatever it was that moved in the darkness seemed always to be ahead of Michael. His short legs were getting tired. Still he pushed on. The night air was cold. Michael pulled the blue blanket tightly around his shoulders. The wind blew dirt and leaves into his eyes, but he kept on walking.

In the darkness, with his eyes half closed against the wind, he did not see the old building until he almost bumped into it. It was an old stable. Seeking shelter at the side of the stable was Michael's missing sheep. Michael reached down and hugged the lost animal. "I will take all of you into this old stable," Michael declared, "we will be warm in there."

Michael's cold little body pushed against the door. It was so bright inside that it was a little while before Michael could see. When his eyes became accustomed to the light, he saw his father and the other shepherds kneeling in front of a manger. There was a little baby in the manger.

Before Michael knelt beside his father, he tiptoed up to the manger and put his blue blanket at the baby's feet. The baby smiled, and Michael understood that the smile meant, "With this small shepherd, I am well pleased."

SS1868

HAMIDA SEES THE STAR

By Edith E. Cutting

Elam, the camel driver, was playing a tune on his flute. "Well, Hamida, little one," he said when he stopped, "are you getting tired?"

Hamida was a baby camel with light brown silky-fuzzy fur. She was only four days old. Elam had named her Hamida when she was born. He thought she was a beautiful little camel.

Early this morning the long line of camels had started its journey. Her mother was in the line, or caravan as Elam called it, and Hamida had been running along beside her.

Now Hamida flopped down on the sand to rest. Quickly Elam and his helper threw a net over her and swung her up onto her mother's back.

At first Hamida kicked and screamed. She didn't know what was happening, and she was scared. Still, she could smell her mother, and that made her feel safe. She quieted down and lay still. Hamida was warm and cozy, rocking along on her mother's back. Soon she was sound asleep.

Every day Hamida got more used to the caravan. She liked to hear the camels' harness bells jingling, especially her mother's. She always knew the special sound of her mother's bells.

Her mother walked near the front of the line and carried a big bundle on her back. There was still room for Hamida, though, when she got tired.

Ahead of Hamida's mother were three other camels. On each one rode a man dressed in a beautiful robe with a big turban to keep the sun off his head. Hamida liked the red and blue and purple colors of their robes. Once she tried to nibble at the edge of one, but the man's camel kicked when she got too near.

Later that day Elam laid a dark green and gold blanket on Hamida's little hump. "There," he said, "now you are dressed as beautifully as those great men who ride ahead."

Hamida was proud of her blanket. She held her head high as she walked along beside her mother.

Shining Star Publications, Copyright © 1988, A Division of Good Apple, Inc. SS1868

At night the caravan stopped for the camels to eat and rest. After the camels were taken care of, the men built little camp fires for themselves.

Usually Hamida just drank milk from her mother, but one night Elam gave her three dates. She nibbled on them and decided they tasted good. She nudged his hand to give her some more.

Elam just smiled. "Not too many at first," he said, "tomorrow I will give you more."

The night got dark very quickly, but there were many little lights up in the sky.

"Stars," said Elam, as he saw Hamida looking up. Just then one of the men who always rode at the head of the caravan lifted his arm and pointed. The others turned to look and began to talk excitedly.

"Ah," said Elam softly, "the wise men are studying the stars." Where the man had pointed was a brighter, shinier star than any of the others.

Hamida watched until she fell asleep. After that, every night at dark she looked for that star, and every night the beautiful star was there.

Two or three times Hamida had seen Elam twisting pieces of leather and fastening them together. One night when the camels had all been fed, and the wise men were looking at the big star, she saw him working on the leather again. She was so curious that she stuck her nose down close to his fingers.

Before she knew what he was doing, he slid the leather straps right over her nose and ears. Hamida screamed and spit at him and ran away. Then he began to jingle a little bell.

"Come back, little Hamida," he called softly. He jingled the bell again and again. It sounded almost like her mother's bells. Finally Hamida came back and stuck out her nose again.

This time Elam hung the bell on one of her straps. Hamida jerked her head back, and the bell tinkled. Every time she moved, it tinkled again. Hamida liked that. Now she had a bell like her mother's, but this one was her very own.

Each night the three men who rode ahead of Hamida's mother studied the stars. Then they sat around their little fire and talked. One night Hamida saw them showing things to each other. Quietly she came closer and looked over their shoulders.

"When the star leads us at last to the new-born king," one man was saying, "I shall give him a present of gold." He held out a handful of shining coins for the others to see.

"That is a royal gift," his friend agreed, "but I have brought frankincense to give. That, too, is costly, and it will smell sweet for the baby." He passed around a little leather bag for the others to sniff.

Then the third man spoke. "I shall give myrrh," he said, "it is a rare perfume." Hamida could smell its bitter spiciness. She wrinkled her nose as she turned away.

"It would be nicer if they had brought dates for the baby," she thought, as she left them and went to find Elam. Perhaps he would give her a handful to chew on.

One morning Hamida was feeling naughty. Elam had slipped a silver ring into her nose. After that, whenever he came near, she would squeal and kick.

"Hamida," he said gently, "I'm sorry the ring hurts but you will soon like it. Your mother has one, you know."

Hamida didn't care. She squealed and kicked again. Then she ran away along the line of camels. Elam called to her, but she paid no attention. She ran so far she could not see her mother any more.

Hamida looked around. She didn't know any of the camels she saw, and none of them paid any attention to her. At last Elam appeared and fastened a thin rope to her new leather headstraps. Hamida squealed, but she was glad to see him just the same. She followed where he led.

When they saw her mother again, Elam untied the rope and gave Hamida a handful of dates. This time she didn't squeal. She was glad to be back and didn't feel naughty any more.

After many days and many nights, the caravan came to a river. "Ah," called one of the wise men, "the great Jordan River!"

The camels all hurried to the edge of the water. They drank and drank, but at last they were ready to cross the river. When it was her turn, Hamida's mother stepped into the water and started to wade across, but Hamida was afraid.

She sniffed at the water. She put one foot in, then pulled it back.

"Go on, little Hamida," urged Elam. "It won't hurt you."

Hamida's mother looked back, jingling her bells, but she did not stop.

Finally Hamida jumped in and started splashing across. The water tickled her legs, and it was cold. When she climbed out on the other bank, she shook herself.

"Now, little Hamida," said Elam, "you have crossed the Jordan River. Next you will see Jerusalem. Who knows what else you will see in your lifetime?" Gently he laid the green and gold blanket over her back, and Hamida felt warm again.

The next day they came to the crowded city. Elam fastened a little rope from Hamida's silver nose-ring to her mother's harness. That way she could not get lost.

Some of the camel drivers stopped their camels by the busy market, and some went down different streets. At last there were left only Hamida, her mother and Elam, and the three other camels with their wise men.

 SS1868

"We must ask where he is, that is born King of the Jews," said one of the men. Hamida watched as they started asking everyone who came by, but nobody knew.

The wise men decided to ride farther into the city. Finally they came to a great big building. "It's Herod's palace," she heard one of the men say, "he will know if a new king has been born."

The other men agreed. They made their camels kneel by the palace and went inside to ask. Hamida tried to go, too, but the little rope held her tight, and she had to wait.

The caravan had to wait two or three days while Herod consulted other wise men, but at last he gave an answer.

When the men came out of the palace that night, Hamida heard one say, "We must go on to Bethlehem."

Another shook his head. "No king would be born in such a little village," he argued.

But the third pointed to the sky. "The star is still moving in that direction. We must follow the star," he said.

Hamida looked up. The beautiful big star was nearer than it had ever been before.

The camels were tired and hungry. They groaned as they lurched up onto their feet. Hamida heard their bells jingling, and she shook her head to make her bell jingle, too.

Then she heard another sound. Elam was playing his flute again. It sounded sweet and clear like another bell. The camels stopped groaning as if they all liked it. One after another they started along the road to Bethlehem.

When they arrived at the edge of the village, the wise men stopped and made the camels kneel so they could get down. Now the beautiful star was shining straight down where they were.

Hamida saw the men open the door of a little building and go in. The other camels stayed kneeling, but Hamida wanted to see where the men had gone. Besides, Elam had not tied her this time. She followed the men to the door. It was unlatched, so she pushed it open a little with her nose.

She could see the three wise men kneeling in front of a baby on a bed of hay. The baby's mother sat by him, and a man stood nearby. Hamida saw the wise men lay their gifts on the floor.

Then she heard the baby's happy gurgling. It sounded as nice as her little bell. Hamida shook her head to hear that ring again, and the baby's mother looked up at her and smiled.

SS1868

THE OX IN THE STABLE

By Katherine D. M. Marko

The ox in the stable stirred. Had morning come so soon? He felt he had scarcely lain down. Yet there was bright light outside. But for some strange reason it did not look like dawn.

He started to rise, wishing there were more hours for sleep. After all, he was no longer young, but he was still strong. That was why he was called the Strong One. He was used to plowing all his life and pulling carts and threshing grain. Now he belonged to the innkeeper here in Bethlehem and hauled supplies for the house. But the day before had been one of the hardest days he ever worked.

His legs were still stiff and his shoulders sore where the yoke had rested. The road back to Bethlehem had been choked by people of all kinds. Many were on foot,

the sick were on pallets and some well-to-do rode on horses or sedan chairs.

By the muttering and complaints along the way, most of them were displeased by a command given by someone called Caesar. It said all citizens had to return to the city of their fathers to be counted.

It was difficult to weave through the crush of travelers. And the stony, uneven places in the road made the cart he pulled jerk and wobble. Often his driver poked him with a long stick urging him to go faster. But how could he, with so many stopping here and there to rest? It was a task just to be careful where his big hooves stomped down. He certainly didn't want to hurt anyone.

He remembered one young couple in particular. The lady sat on a small donkey, hunched over as though very tired. It was

SS1868

at a rise in the road where one could see Jerusalem in the distance. The husband was looking out towards the city with wonder in his eyes. Then the Strong One's driver shouted roughly, "You there, move to one side. The road is not only for you."

The lady looked around, startled, and called out in a kind tone, "Joseph, we must go. We are in the way."

The young man came quickly to the side of the donkey. He nodded to the Strong One's driver. "I am sorry," he said, and, catching up the lead rope, he led the donkey along.

As the lady pulled her blue robe about her, the Strong One could see that a great deal of dust had worked itself into the clothes of the young couple. They must have come a long way. At a wider spot in the road they drew to one side. There was something very unforgettable about them, the Strong One felt as he plodded on past.

It was well after sunset when he finally pulled the rough, rattling cart up to the inn. There the confusion was the same. Tired, impatient people were milling about, seeking shelter. There seemed to be no room anywhere. The Strong One felt sorry for these travelers with nowhere to go. He was glad when the driver led him along the path beside the inn down to the stable beneath it. A few sheep and a skinny goat were there ahead of him resting in the shadows. After he had eaten some of the hay in the manger, he bent his knees and lowered his bulky body with a huge sigh. How good it would be to sleep.

But now he had already awakened and the light outside was growing brighter and brighter. He lumbered to his feet and plodded to the low doorway. A gust of cold night air swept over him. Squinting the sleep from his eyes, he looked up at the sky. It was still dark and, instead of the sun, he saw a great, golden star overhead. This certainly was not dawn. A shiver rippled the dun-colored skin of his shoulders all the way back to his flanks. There was something strange and different about this night—something awfully and wonderfully different.

The Strong One went back to his place. The star's light seemed to come right into the stable. He could see the lady clearly. She used her blue cloak as a coverlet and her long, dark hair spread back from her face. She was very beautiful. She moved and the straw rustled.

The Strong One bent his knees and lay down. Feeling that his curiosity was rude, he turned his face away and closed his eyes.

All at once there was a great rustling of the straw—then quiet. At the doorway the man called in, "I have brought the water."

The lady answered, "Come in, Joseph." Her voice was low.

The next moment the Strong One heard a thin, little sound. It was a wailing sound like a baby's cry. A baby! The Strong One couldn't resist looking. Yes, it was a newborn child. The man took it clumsily in his arms and the lady wrapped long white cloths around it. Then tenderly, they laid it in the manger.

A baby! The Strong One couldn't get over it. He rose to his feet again and moved closer. He saw the child's face, a little face like any other baby's, yet so different he could never describe it.

A soft bleating came from the sheep and goat. And there were voices again at the doorway. Joseph was ushering in some shy, hesitant men. They were shepherds. The Strong One could smell the sheep on their clothing. One was explaining about a king being born this night in the town of David. "And the angels said, 'As a sign you will find an infant wrapped in swaddling clothes and lying in a manger.' " Then they knelt down to adore the child.

A king, they said. This child was a king! And angels had sung about this place— his stable? But why would a king be born in a cave that sheltered common beasts?

There around the corner of the stable came a man leading a donkey. On its back sat a figure hunched over. The man, very tenderly and carefully, lifted down the form. It was that of a woman.

"Oh, Mary," the man was saying, "I am sorry indeed to bring you to a stable." His voice was full of sadness.

The lady clung to his arm as he helped her through the doorway. "Don't worry, Joseph," she said, "It is shelter."

They were the young couple he had seen on the road. When the lady finally lay down on the straw to rest, the man cleaned out the manger. Then putting fresh hay in it, he covered the hay with a blanket.

That was odd, the Strong One thought.

"I will get some water," the man said. "Will you be all right, Mary?"

She nodded wearily. "Yes, Joseph, I will be fine."

Things were becoming more strange each moment. How he wished he had something to offer as a gift. But he was just a poor ox. What could he give?

When the shepherds left, the lady sighed. "It is comfortable here," she said, "the warmth of the animals is good." She looked around gratefully and her glance rested on the Strong One.

Warmth of the animals? Oh, how happy her words made him feel. He was giving something. He did not go back to his usual place but stayed as close to the manger as he could.

During the following days many visitors came to the stable. Among them were three richly-clad men on camels. They brought gifts of gold, frankincense and myrrh, and spoke about seeing King Herod on their way here. They looked like kings themselves.

By this time the Strong One felt as if he belonged to the family in the stable more than to the innkeeper. He was hoping they would stay forever. He could never get enough of watching the child in the manger. When he was out working he couldn't wait until the day was over. He almost galloped in his hurry to get back. Every night he stayed as near to the three as possible so that his breath and warmth would make them comfortable. He always felt there was fondness in the lady's eyes when she looked at him.

Then one day he found them preparing to leave. "We must go to Egypt," the man was saying, "for the safety of the child."

With a look of sadness, the lady nodded willingly.

"But, oh," the Strong One thought, "who will give them warmth out on the road these cold nights?" And how would he bear not being able to see the child anymore? He wished he could go with them, but that was not possible.

The next morning at dawn they left quietly. The Strong One stood at the low doorway with a heavy heart. Tears stung his large, round eyes as he watched them disappear out of sight.

He knew he would never see them again.

Then he turned sadly back into the stable. How empty it was now. He nosed the straw lovingly and lay his big face against the manger.

He knew for the rest of his life that he would never look up at a night sky again without remembering the huge golden star that hung over this place when the child was born.

No, nothing in this stable would ever be the same again, for something great and wonderful had touched him here.

CHRISTMAS CHORAL READINGS

CHORAL READING TIPS

by Helen Kitchell Evans

Choral speaking as a vocal activity dates back five-hundred years before the birth of Christ. In Greek drama, the odes were recited or chanted with accompanying body movements. The revival of CHORAL READING is receiving wide acceptance in the modern classroom. Its value as a form of artistic expression has innumerable benefits. It is fun and it certainly increases the love of poetry. It helps the timid to develop while restraining the aggressive. It establishes confidence within the group. Greatest of all, it improves speech. If you have been wanting to begin a speaking choir, don't hesitate. The selections found on the following pages will provide you with entertainment and an opportunity to advance individuals through group participation.

The organization is not difficult and even the smallest group can enjoy the fun that comes from speaking together. A choir may include as few as eight or a hundred or more. The leader is an important part of the organization. The leader should have a sense of rhythm and some knowledge of interpretation.

There are many ways to present choral readings:

1. The group (if large enough) may be divided into Choir 1 and Choir 2, each speaking certain assigned parts, then the entire group speaks on Chorus. Short poems are best suited to this type.

2. Line-a-child is more difficult as the timing must be perfect from one person to the next.

3. Part-speaking is used when different groups take parts of the selection.

4. Solo and Chorus uses various members of the group speaking certain lines and then they join together on the chorus. This can be a recitation format and works well with small children.

5. Unison speaking is the most difficult type of choral reading. This means that the entire group speaks as one person. This requires perfect timing, balance, phrasing and harmony in inflection. Not to be performed in sing-song fashion!

The standard procedure in presentation of choral selections is as follows:

1. The leader speaks the selection as it should be presented. Then it is repeated line by line to see if the meaning is grasped by the group.

2. The leader speaks the selection again having the group read along silently, if they are of reading age. If not, have them repeat each line orally. Encourage wide open mouth movements.

3. Solo parts may be assigned here (if desired).

4. Memorization is required before proceeding if this is to be a presentation before an audience. Give each child a copy of the readings you will be performing.

Staging may take various forms:

1. Choir may be placed in rows on risers (if group is large) with arms at sides. If solo parts have been assigned, place high voices on the left, medium in the center and low on the right. Small children do not have enough variance in voice range for the division to be based on voice tone.

2. With a smaller group have choir stand shoulder to shoulder with arms behind them. Each speaker steps forward, presents his/her selection and then steps back into place.

It is advisable for the leader to stand before the group (as with a singing choir) and direct. All eyes should stay fixed on the director who speaks the words with all facial expressions silently. This helps keep the group together. However, if the group is small and each person is to speak alone, the director may be seated in front and stand only when the entire group speaks in unison. HAPPY DIRECTING! IT'S GREAT FUN!

Shining Star Publications, Copyright © 1988, A Division of Good Apple, Inc.

SS1868

THE TWELVE WONDERS OF JESUS

by Mary A. Magers
(Sung to: "Twelve Days of Christmas")

All:	1.	In the story of my Savior the Bible says to me: That His salvation is free.
All:	2.	In the story of my Savior the Bible says to me:
Group 1:		Angels announced His birth, and
All:		That His salvation is free.
All:	3.	In the story of my Savior the Bible says to me:
Group 2:		When 12 He spoke in the temple,
Group 1:		Angels announced His birth, and
All:		That His salvation is free.
All:	4.	In the story of my Savior the Bible says to me:
Group 3:		That God's dove blessed His baptism,
Group 2:		When 12 He spoke in the temple,
Group 1:		Angels announced His birth, and
All:		That His salvation is free.
All:	5.	In the story of my Savior the Bible says to me: That everyone should pray.
Group 3:		God's dove blessed His baptism,
Group 2:		When 12 He spoke in the temple,
Group 1:		Angels announced His birth, and
All:		That His salvation is free.
All:	6.	In the story of my Savior the Bible says to me:
Group 4:		That Jesus chose 12 disciples.
All:		Everyone should pray.
Group 3:		God's dove blessed His baptism,
Group 2:		When 12 He spoke in the temple,
Group 1:		Angels announced His birth, and
All:		That His salvation is free.
All:	7.	In the story of my Savior the Bible says to me:
Group 5:		That Jesus fed five thousand,
Group 4:		Jesus chose 12 disciples.
All:		Everyone should pray.
Group 3:		God's dove blessed His baptism,
Group 2:		When 12 He spoke in the temple,
Group 1:		Angels announced His birth, and
All:		That His salvation is free.
All:	8.	In the story of my Savior the Bible says to me:
Group 6:		That Jesus walked on water,
Group 5:		Jesus fed five thousand,
Group 4:		Jesus chose 12 disciples.
All:		Everyone should pray.
Group 3:		God's dove blessed His baptism,
Group 2:		When 12 He spoke in the temple,
Group 1:		Angels announced His birth, and
All:		That His salvation is free.

SS1868

All:	9.	In the story of my Savior the Bible says to me:
Group 7:		That Jesus raised up Lazarus,
Group 6:		Jesus walked on water,
Group 5:		Jesus fed five thousand,
Group 4:		Jesus chose 12 disciples.
All:		Everyone should pray.
Group 3:		God's dove blessed His baptism,
Group 2:		When 12 He spoke in the temple,
Group 1:		Angels announced His birth, and
All:		That His salvation is free.

All:	10.	In the story of my Savior the Bible says to me:
Group 8:		That palms were spread before Him,
Group 7:		Jesus raised up Lazarus,
Group 6:		Jesus walked on water,
Group 5:		Jesus fed five thousand,
Group 4:		Jesus chose 12 disciples.
All:		Everyone should pray.
Group 3:		God's dove blessed His baptism,
Group 2:		When 12 He spoke in the temple,
Group 1:		Angels announced His birth, and
All:		That His salvation is free.

All:	11.	In the story of my Savior the Bible says to me:
Group 9:		That Jesus died for others,
Group 8:		Palms were spread before Him,
Group 7:		Jesus raised up Lazarus,
Group 6:		Jesus walked on water,
Group 5:		Jesus fed five thousand,
Group 4:		Jesus chose 12 disciples.
All:		Everyone should pray.
Group 3:		God's dove blessed His baptism,
Group 2:		When 12 He spoke in the temple,
Group 1:		Angels announced His birth, and
All:		That His salvation is free.

All:	12.	In the story of my Savior the Bible says to me:
Group 10:		That Jesus rose triumphant,
Group 9:		That Jesus died for others,
Group 8:		Palms were spread before Him,
Group 7:		Jesus raised up Lazarus,
Group 6:		Jesus walked on water,
Group 5:		Jesus fed five thousand,
Group 4:		Jesus chose 12 disciples.
All:		Everyone should pray.
Group 3:		God's dove blessed His baptism,
Group 2:		When 12 He spoke in the temple,
Group 1:		Angels announced His birth, and
All:		That His salvation is free.

Lacking sufficient numbers, one might alternate boy and girl groups throughout, or some other convenient division.

Shining Star Publications, Copyright © 1988, A Division of Good Apple, Inc.   SS1868

JUST LIKE ME

by Louise Hannah Kohr

All respond:

Child 1:   When Jesus was a boy
I think He raised his eyes
To the wonder of
The stars and skies.

                Just like me!

Child 2:   When Jesus was a boy
I think He watched the birds
And listened to them sing,
Thanking God for everything.

                Just like me!

Child 3:   When Jesus was a boy
I'm sure He loved the flowers
That made the world so fair,
Spreading beauty everywhere.

                Just like me!

Child 4:   When Jesus was a boy
I think He loved the morning light,
And thanked God for the lovely day
And for the rest of night.

                Just like me!

Child 5:   When Jesus was a boy
I think He loved the little things,
Violets and butterflies
And ladybugs with spotted wings.

                Just like me!

Child 6:   When Jesus was a boy
I'm sure He shared
With those in need
Because He cared.

                Just like me!

Child 7:   When Jesus was a boy
I think He thanked God for things that grow,
For the promise of His love
In the bright rainbow.

                Just like me!

Child 8:   When Jesus was a boy
I think He liked to sit at his mother's knee,
And listen to her tell stories
Of God's love.

                Just like me!

Child 9:   When Jesus was a boy
I'm sure He knelt to pray,
To thank His heavenly Father
For each newborn day.

                Just like me!

DON'T FORGET

by Helen Kitchell Evans

Chorus has red ribbons tied on pointing fingers.
Chorus shakes their fingers during their lines.

Choir 1:	Let's enjoy the beauty Of a lovely Christmas tree,
Choir 2:	Let's enjoy the friendship Of friends and family.
Chorus:	But let's keep Christ in Christmas That all the world might see.
Choir 1:	Let's enjoy our presents We find on Christmas morn
Choir 2:	And let's always remember The night Jesus was born.
Chorus:	But let's keep Christ in Christmas That all the world might see.
Choir 1:	Let's enjoy the carols And all the songs we hear;
Choir 2:	Let's enjoy the pretty lights We see this time of year;
Chorus:	But let's keep Christ in Christmas That all the world might see.
Choir 1:	Let's make this a wonderful season Filled with laughter and with joy.
Choir 2:	Let us never forget Jesus, Mary's baby boy.
Chorus:	Yes, let's keep Christ in Christmas That all the world might see.

SS1868

THE JOYS OF CHRISTMAS

by Helen Kitchell Evans

Child 1: ✓

The thing that I like about Christmas
Is the warmth we feel together;
Sunny or snowy it's always the same,
Christmas is great in all kinds of weather.

Child 2: ✓

I like the suspense of Christmas
The mystery in the air;
The way my family and friends
Enjoy laughter and love and prayer.

Child 3:

The cookies of Christmas are special,
My mother bakes for days;
Little animals and trees,
Even cookies sing God's praise.

Child 4: ✓

Many blessings come to us
When Christmas time is here;
But we receive daily blessings
Not just at this time of year.

Child 5: ✓

Grandmother comes to our house
Many times throughout the year,
But it seems so extra special
When Christmastime is here.

Child 6: ✓

My mother says I'm sneaky,
I'm too inquisitive;
But if I peep a little
I hope she will forgive.

Child 7: ✓

Just think—there will always be a Christmas
Given to us by a special birth;
The birth of dear Jesus, our Savior,
Who came down from heaven to earth.

The child that is speaking can step forward holding a banner with the appropiate word written on it.

SS1868

Child 8: The tiny lights that twinkle
Upon the Christmas tree
Add a glow of happiness
So wonderful to see.

Child 9: I guess I'm about the smallest
But I am big in love.
I can sing of my Savior
Who blessed me from above.

Child 10: The thing I like about Christmas
Well—*(Pause.)* it's the presents that appear;
Who wouldn't want to be a child
At this time of the year.

Child 11: Daddy said, "You can."
Mother said, "You should."
So I am here to tell you
"At Christmas I'll be good."

Child 12: Why is it that at Christmas
The church bells sound so clear?
I think it's the Christmas story
That they report each year.

Child 13: Oh, wonderful, wonderful Savior
We sing of glory to you;
Bless each one of your children,
Help us in all that we do.

Child 14: I thought—*(Pause.)* a recitation?
I'll be shaky in my knees;
But it hasn't been bad at all;
See, I've done it with great ease!
MERRY CHRISTMAS!

Child 15: Happy time, Christmas time,
Hearts so full of cheer;
Merry Christmas to all of you. *(Pause.) (Extend arms to side.)*
We're so pleased that you are here. *(Extend hands forward.)*

SS1868

THIS CHRISTMAS SEASON

by Helen Kitchell Evans

This selection should not be rushed back and forth between the two choirs. Let the words be spoken clearly and with eloquence. Let there be a pause between the words spoken by each choir. These words express many kinds of feeling. Try to get the choirs to express that feeling as they speak.

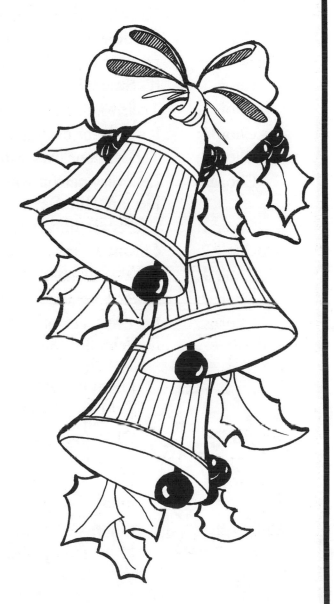

Choir 1:	How joyfully!
Choir 2:	How blessedly!
Chorus:	Comes this Christmas season.
Choir 1:	How splendidly!
Choir 2:	How marvelously!
Chorus:	Christ is the real true reason.
Choir 1:	How silently!
Choir 2:	How carefully!
Chorus:	The shepherds find the place.
Choir 1:	How reverently!
Choir 2:	How humbly!
Chorus:	They look on Jesus' face.
Choir 1:	How elegantly!
Choir 2:	How proudly!
Chorus:	The wise men ride from afar.
Choir 1:	How miraculously!
Choir 2:	How gloriously!
Chorus:	Shines that Christmas star.
Choir 1:	How joyfully!
Choir 2:	How blessedly!
Chorus:	Comes this Christmas season.
Choir 1:	How splendidly!
Choir 2:	How marvelously!
Chorus:	Christ is the real true reason.

Shining Star Publications, Copyright © 1988, A Division of Good Apple, Inc.

SS1868

THE STRANGER

by Helen Kitchell Evans

Choir 1:   In a manger was a stranger
We call the Prince of Peace;

Choir 2:   Let us love and honor Him
Let our prayers never cease.

Choir 1:   Around the bed of new mown hay
The shepherds stood with silent gaze;

Choir 2:   The wise men, too, had come
To offer gifts of praise.

Chorus: Let every person with joyful voice
Declare Him Savior and rejoice!

Choir 1:   It's time for bells to chime,

Choir 2:   Their sounds truly bless;

Choir 1:   It's time for carols to be heard,

Choir 2:   They fill our lives with happiness.

Chorus: Let every person with joyful voice
Declare Him Savior and rejoice!

Choir 1:   Hearts are filled with joy.

Choir 2:   Christmastime is here;

Choir 1:   What a wonderful season!

Choir 2:   What a wonderful time of year!

Chorus: Let every person with joyful voice
Declare Him Savior and rejoice!

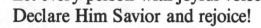

Shining Star Publications, Copyright © 1988, A Division of Good Apple, Inc.

SS1868

FOR EVERYONE!

by Kay Tira

VOICE:		ACTION:
ALL:	The wise men	(Point to head.)
ALL:	Saw the star You sent	(Wiggle fingers up high, like stars twinkling.)
ALL:	You told them of Your Son . . .	(Fold arms in front of body, as if holding baby.)
ALL:	They followed	(March in place, or walk a few steps in single file.)
ALL:	And brought gifts to Him	(Hold hands out together, palms-up, as if holding gift out.)
ALL:	He came for everyone!	(Point to individuals in audience—one, two, three.)

NO ROOM! NO ROOM?

by Kay Tira

GIRLS: A child asleep in his mother's arms,
so wee, so still, and helpless . . .

BOYS: Men bearing gifts came from afar
amazed, in awe, and selfless.

ALL: There was no room for the mom with child.
The people turned them out!

GIRLS: But a quiet, gentle Spirit spoke,
and the parents had no doubt.

BOYS: This child will grow and love and live.
He's come to save the world!

ALL: No room! No room? They just don't know
The secret will be unfurled.

BOYS: And time will tell, soon all will
see this Child—HE IS THE
CHRIST!

GIRLS: Helpless? No, not He, the Son—
He came once . . . soon TWICE!

SS1868

A SPECIAL GIFT

by Kay Tira

Girls: You gave me Lord Jesus
Boys: On that special Christmas Day.
All: Help me to love Him
With the things that I say.

Girls: Jesus was a gift to us—
Boys: You sent Him with your love.
All: We want to serve Him all our lives
And live with You, above.

Girls: You gave me Lord Jesus,
Boys: Your only begotten Son!
All: Now He lives in my heart—
What a wonderful thing You've done!

Girls: Thank You, Father,
Boys: For loving us so much.
All: We celebrate Christmas
With your special touch.

Girls: He came as a baby,
Boys: And grew, just like me!
All: He had a special mission
When He died upon the tree.

Girls: And You brought Him back to life again,
Boys: So that we could live.
All: What a special present
Only God can give!

SS1868

WONDERFUL CHRISTMAS

A musical choral reading presentation
by Helen Kitchell Evans

INTROIT: ADESTE FIDELES

Speaker 1:   Daddy said, "Bah, Humbug!"
And I heard Mother say,
"Now _____ change your attitude
Upon this blessed day."

He did, and you know what?
He stopped his blustering sound
And from that time he was
Real nice to have around!

Speaker 2:   It's such a nice time of the year
When unkindness ceases,
And "MERRY CHRISTMAS" fills the air
And goodwill increases.

Speaker 3:   Grandma often talks about
Christmas of long ago
When she rode behind a horse
Across the fallen snow.

Speaker 4:   It must have been quite wonderful
To travel in this way;
To go to church on Christmas
In an open sleigh.

SONG:
I HEARD THE BELLS ON CHRISTMAS
DAY

SS1868

Speaker 4: I've been trying lately
To be a better boy,
For Christmastime is near
And I want to bring folks joy.

My mother does appreciate;
She says that I'm a dear,
But that I should consider
Being good throughout the year.

Speaker 5: It is when you give of yourself
That you truly give.
This is the way
That I'm trying to live.

At Christmastime
And all through the year,
I am trying to scatter
Sunshine and cheer.

Speaker 6: I love the Christmas season
With candles all aglow;
With smell of pine in the air—
The story we love so.

The story of dear Jesus
And how He came to earth;
So wonderful is this story
Of our Savior's birth.

SONG: ANGELS WE HAVE HEARD ON HIGH

Speaker 7: Lord, comfort those who are ill
We know not what the reason,
But give them extra blessings
At this Christmas season.

May the star that shone that night
Still shine for them today;
Bless all your children, Lord,
Hear us as we pray.

SS1868

Speaker 8:   Oh, the joy of Christmas morning
When the church bells ring with joy,
Announcing once again
The birth of a baby boy.

May we this Christmas morning
Like those wise men of old
Stand at His manger, too,
With our myrrh, frankincense and gold.

SONG: AWAY IN A MANGER

Speaker 9:   *(With the group or as a special recitation.)*

I'VE LIVED TO HELP

If I have proved a friend
To someone in need today,
If I have helped another
In a special kind of way,
If I have cheered one lonely
In a lonely little place,
If I have shown by giving
That I take my Christian place;
Then this day has been well spent.
I've shown God walks with me;
I've lived to help my fellowman
As God intended life to be.

SONG: GO TELL IT ON THE MOUNTAIN

Chorus: Wonderful, wonderful season!
We kneel in adoration!
May love for everyone
Flow from nation to nation!

SS1868

ECHO PRAISE

by Patty Medill

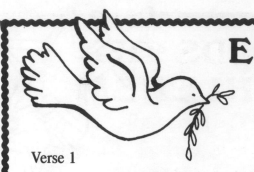

Verse 1

Narrator: Hear the promise of a King;
Listen to the angels sing,
Call Him Jesus!

Response: Call Him Jesus!

Narrator: See proud Joseph stand and smile;
Mary wants to watch awhile,
Baby Jesus!

Response: Baby Jesus!

Narrator: Smell the hay that blessed morn,
Helping keep the Savior warm,
In a manger!

Response: In a manger!

Narrator: Touch the lamb as white as snow,
Brought by shepherds meek and low,
Sent by angels!

Response: Sent by angels!

Narrator: Taste the spices rich and sweet,
Laid in wonder at His feet.
Wise men worship!

Response: Wise men worship!

Verse 2

Narrator: Taste the birthday cake we bring,
Baked to honor that same King.
Honor Jesus!

Response: Honor Jesus!

Narrator: Touch the gifts wrapped up so
bright;
In memory of God's gift that night,
Thank you, Father!

Response: Thank you, Father!

Narrator: Smell the incense as we share;
Others need to know and care.
Sharing Jesus!

Response: Sharing Jesus!

Narrator: See us raise our hearts and hands,
Wise men still throughout the lands,
Worship Jesus!

Response: Worship Jesus!

Narrator: Hear our joyful sound we pray;
Jesus reigns supreme today!
Let us praise Him!

Response: Let us praise Him!

Narrator: Let us praise Him!

Response: Let us praise Him!

Narrator: King Jesus!

Response: King Jesus!

(One sharp clap ends the reading.)

This choral reading can have appropriate
actions added, and the narrator's part may
be read by several different children.

SS1868

GOLDS OF BETHLEHEM

by Edith E. Cutting

Boy's voice:	Gold of shepherd's flickering fire,
Girl's voice:	Gold of sparkling star,
Boy's voice:	Golden straw in stable bed For family from afar.
Girl's voice:	Coins of gold from king in robe With gold-embroidered hem,
Boy's voice:	Gold of simple candle flame—
Both:	(All) golds of Bethlehem.

THROUGHOUT THE YEAR

by Helen Kitchell Evans

Echo - Side → Side   1st

First child:	When we have a cheerful heart We give cheer to others;
Second child:	We have a happier family With our parents, sisters and brothers.
Third child:	A cheerful heart is good medicine So take a big dose every day;
Fourth child:	Gladden the hearts of everyone For this is the only way.
Fifth child:	Don't let Christmas be the only time When there is great love and cheer,
All:	Keep the Christmas spirit alive Within the family throughout the year.

(Try something a little different in your program and add Bible verses with your message. With the above have a child read the following verse from the Bible before the children recite the verse.)

"A merry heart doeth good like a medicine: but a broken spirit drieth the bones."

Proverbs 17:22

SS1868

ONE SPECIAL STAR

by Edith E. Cutting

Child 1: The world was dark;

Child 2: The night was still;

Child 1: A few small stars
Shone on the hill.

Child 2: One special star
Gave brilliant light;

Child 1: One special song
Rang sweet that night.

Together: So we celebrate
With light and song

That manger birth,
Our whole life long.

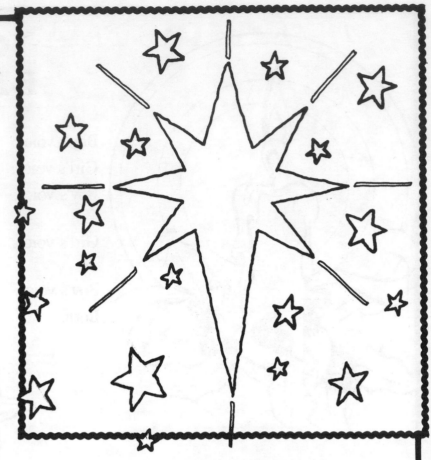

ISN'T IT NICE

by Helen Kitchell Evans

Choir 1: Isn't it nice at Christmas
To have friends around once more?

Choir 2: Isn't it nice to greet relatives
At the old home door?

Choir 1: Isn't it nice to listen
To carolers as they sing?

Choir 2: Isn't it wonderful to know
Of the blessed Savior, our King?

Choir 1: Isn't it nice to feel
The wonder of Christmas night?

Choir 2: Isn't it wonderfutl that He
Is still the Christmas light?

Chorus: Christmas, the mystery of Christmas,
Fills the heart with love;
Brings us ever closer
To the Savior up above.

SS1868

CHRISTMAS POEMS
AND SONGS SUNG NEW

POETRY FOR PLEASURE

by Helen Kitchell Evans

Probably no nation provides as much literature for children as does the United States, yet many of our children are not reading up to their potential. If literature is to be an exhilarating educational experience, teachers need to be enthusiastic about the presentation. This is especially true of poetry. This form of dramatic interpretation requires that the teacher be sensitive to voice inflection, mood and rhythm.

Children enjoy poetry which is closely related to their thoughts, feelings, images and perception of their own world of experience. They like poems that tell stories, make them laugh, nonsense rhymes, and poems which present pictures of beauty.

By the time a child arrives at school, he/she has most likely begun to enjoy the rhythm of verses through hearing and learning the nursery rhymes. He/she often asks to have the same selection repeated time and again.

When the child arrives at school he/she should be encouraged to write "poems" even if it is only two lines that rhyme.

No program in literature is complete without many hours of poetry. It enriches the day's living and sings its way into the minds and memories of children.

When children come to school filled with the love of rhythm, their senses attuned for the acceptance of poetry, what a shame if their inclinations are killed. Some schools fail to kindle this art form. Too often poetry becomes a dull assignment instead of joy. Poetry loses its flavor when it becomes a routine task.

The difference between poetry and recitation is quite obvious. Poetry is for the joy of learning and recitation for the joy of an audience.

Before reading poetry in the classroom ask yourself this question: Does this poem have something to say to the children? Can they relate to its meaning? Will it touch the mind and spirit?

Since nursery tunes are so familiar, children are delighted to try new words to the tunes that have already become a part of their musical background. Turn to pages 48-50 and you will have fun with these new words to the old tunes.

SS1868

JESUS' BIRTH

by Lucille B. Golphenee

Many long years ago, Jesus came down,
And was born as a baby, in Bethlehem town.
   The stars in the heavens shone brightly that night,
   As they twinkled and blinked at the wonderful sight.
Mary, His mother and Joseph, had come—
Their taxes to pay—which must surely be done.
   No room was there found for the Lord at the inn—
   The Saviour of earth—the Redeemer from sin.
So He slept with the cattle—a manger, His bed—
As He lay down in peace, His dear little head.
   There came from the east, three wise men, afar—
   To see the new King—and they followed His star.
Frankincense and myrrh, and gold, they did bring,
And gave to Him there, as they worshipped the King.
   And shepherds there were, in the country nearby,
   When the glory of heaven shone down from the sky.
Then they trembled and shook, with fear and with dread,
But the angel of God came upon them, and said—
   "Fear not, for I bring you glad tidings of joy—
   For in Bethlehem town, is a new baby boy—
The Messiah, foretold both by tongue, and by pen—
Redeemer for all—and the Savior of men.
   And this be your sign—you shall find the wee stranger
   In swaddling clothes wrapped, and His bed is a manger."
Then came a great host of bright angels, to say,
"All glory to God, and on earth—peace—today."
   When the angels were gone, the shepherds all went
   To see the new King, who from heaven was sent.
And when they had found Him, they told it abroad—
So joyful were they—and gave praises to God.

SS1868

THEY WERE THE MAGI

By Katherine D. M. Marko

From far off they traveled
Across sandy drifts
Of deserts on camels,
All bearing great gifts.

On reaching the stable,
They knelt to adore
The Babe who was born
To be king evermore.

The wise men then gave Him
The gifts that they brought,
All thankful for finding
The God whom they sought.

CHRISTMAS IS HERE

by Helen Kitchell Evans

Christmas is here.
A time for the singing of carols,
An enchanting time of sharing,
A time of truly caring.
A time of family gatherings,
A time for remembering the past,
Memories of happy childhood
Stored in the crevices of the mind.
Wonderful love, sincere and kind.
Crocheted stars on a pretty tree,
Grandmother made them just for me,
Smiles of those we all hold dear,
Love everywhere
Christmas is here.
Peace and joy floats over the earth
As we celebrate the humble birth;
A magic, awesome time,
Days filled with cheer,
Christmas is here.

SS1868

DOWN FROM NAZARETH

by Katherine D. M. Marko

Down from Nazareth, amid the crowd
Mary and Joseph, weary and bowed,
Journeyed with others to David's town
Obeying the order from Caesar's crown.

Down from Nazareth to Bethlehem,
They, Scripture tells, made way for Him.
Down dusty roads to the sheltered cave
Where, in a manger, God, to us, gave
The Prince of Peace with all of His love
While an angel chorus sounded above
The lonely hillside where shepherds lay,
Announcing to all our first Christmas Day.

GIFTS FOR THE CHILD

by Edith E. Cutting

If gold you have,
Then gold you give
To help a newborn
Child to live.

And frankincense
Or myrrh will do,
If these are what
You have with you.

But greater gifts
Than all of these
Are wond'ring eyes
And bended knees.

SS1868

CHRISTMAS

by Eileen Horning Weaver

I love to hear about Christmas
When Jesus, our Savior was born.
To think He lay in a stable
On that first Christmas morn.

The shepherds heard the message
From angels brought to earth,
As they sang the joyous tidings
Of baby Jesus' birth.

A star led the wise men
As they traveled through the night.
They came with gifts to worship Him
On that first Christmas night.

As Mary and Joseph watched o'er Him,
He slept on a bed of hay,
Wrapped up in swaddling clothes
On that first Christmas Day.

IN A MANGER

by Louise Hannah Kohr

"Away in a manger
No room for a bed,
The little Lord Jesus
Lay down His sweet head."

Sometimes, as baby's will,
He cried, the Holy Child,
But other times I like to think
He pat-a-caked and smiled.

SS1868

WE SEE THE STAR

by Philip Rosenbaum

As prophets long had spoken,
You called us from afar,
And gave us as Your token
A bright and shining star;

And precious gifts You gave us,
To each a different one,
For Him who came to save us,
Your darling only Son.

Across the desert wild
Of this dark fallen world,
We sought your holy Child
While round us tempests whirled.

Up through great mountain ranges
Of peaks so cold and high
Their beauty never changes
And danger's always nigh—

Up there the star shone clearer,
And we found peace of mind,
Knowing it led us nearer
To Him we longed to find.

But we were glad to rest
When this great prince received us;
We told him of our quest—
And knew not he deceived us:

(To make us wise of soul
You put him in our path:
When wise men near their goal
They meet the king of wrath.)

With dazzling lights he fools us
And says your star grows dim;
By subtlety he rules us,
Till we are helping him.

But have we come so far
To serve the evil one?
Where is the shining star
Which leads us to Your Son?

Forgive us, Lord, we pray
For trusting much in men,
And guide us in the way
Lest we should sin again.

Now in the dead of night
We flee his palace dark,
And pray to see the light
That is our Maker's mark.

But will our sin still mar
Our search to find the Boy?
Behold! We see the star
With great, exceeding joy!

SS1868

CHRISTMAS LEGENDS

by Katherine D. M. Marko

They say that in the forest
There's a hush on Christmas Eve
As though each forest creature
Is saying, "I believe."

They say that in the stables
Farm animals can speak
At just one special moment
If no human beings peek.

There also is a legend
Of the donkey Mary rode—
While he carried her, his hoofprints
Were of gold upon the road.

These stories being legends
Cannot be proven true,
But like tiny, bobbing lanterns
They still keep shining through.

When the season's rush grows weighty
And our senses seem to blur,
These legends come as bits of
Gold, frankincense and myrrh.

CHRISTMAS QUESTIONS

by Joan Rae Mills

If Jesus would come
    as a baby today,
Would He have better luck
    finding some place to stay?

Would He be born
    on the poor side of town
After all the motels
    would have turned Him down?

And when the angels announced
    the glorious news,
Would I be one
    of the folks they would choose

To hear it and see them,
    and then would I
Drop all I was doing
    and rush to His side?

I like to think
    that I'd be the one
Who'd believe from the start
    in God's newborn Son.

SS1868

THE HOLY BABE

by Katherine D. M. Marko

The star was shining brightly,
Shepherds heard the angels sing;
They told them that a Babe was born,
That He was Christ the King.

His birthplace was a stable,
His mattress was some hay,
His cradle was a manger
Upon that Christmas Day.

But though He had no riches,
He had all a baby's charms,
All of Joseph's loving heart
And Mary's loving arms.

ONE BRIGHT STAR

by Wanda E. Brunstetter

Have you ever looked into the sky,
And seen the stars up there so high?
They shine like diamonds shiny bright,
Like golden, twinkly, little lights.
Though they are all great to behold,
None can compare to that one star bright
    and bold.
This star was placed for all to see,
To know exactly where the new King would
    be.
Once the brightest Christmas star ever made,
Was placed over Bethlehem, and there it
    stayed.
So when you look at stars on high,
Remember our Lord is always close by.

SS1868

JESUS IS BORN

by Helen Kitchell Evans
Sung to "Frère Jacques"

And she brought forth,
Yes, she brought forth
Her dear son,
Her dear son.
Placed him in a manger,
Shielded him from danger,
Her first son,
Her first son.

In that country,
In that country,
In a field,
In a field,
Shepherds stood by watching;
Shepherds stood by watching,
Through the night,
Through the night.

Lo, the angel
Of the Lord came
Down to earth,
Down to earth.
Glory shone around them,
Brightly shone around them.
They were afraid.
They were afraid.

Then the angel
Said unto them,
"What you see
Was foretold.
Now I bring glad tidings,
Tidings to all people
Fear not, shepherds,
Behold."

In the city
Known as David,
Jesus Christ is now born.
Peace on earth to all men.
Glory in the highest,
Christ is born,
Christ is born.

GO SCATTER LOVE AND SUNSHINE

by Helen Kitchell Evans
Sung to "Go Tell It on the Mountain"

Verse:

In all the world are people
Who cry out for our love,
Who never heard of Jesus
And His forgiving love.

Chorus:

Go scatter love and sunshine
Over the hills and everywhere;
Go scatter love and sunshine
To people everywhere.

(Sing through once, facing congregation. Then children go into the congregation, shaking hands or hugging friends as desired.)

SS1868

CHRISTMAS DAY

by Helen Kitchell Evans
Sung to: "Frère Jacques"

First child sings:

Infant Jesus
Infant Jesus
Born this night,
Born this night,
With your grace and mercy
With your grace and mercy
Lead me right,
Lead me right.

All children sing:

On this Christmas
On this Christmas
Hear us say,
Hear us say,
Love and honor to you,
Love and honor to you
Christmas Day,
Christmas Day.

Second child sings:

Savior Jesus
Savior Jesus
Be with me,
Be with me,
Give me many blessings
Give me many blessings
Be with me,
Be with me.

Third child sings:

Gentle Jesus
Gentle Jesus
Lead my way,
Lead my way,
Help me to show kindness
Help me to show kindness
Every day,
Every day.

SS1868

CHRISTMAS

by Helen Kitchell Evans
Sung to: "We've a Story to Tell"

We've a story to tell to all races,
It's a story of God's great love,
A story of how Jesus came here
From heaven up above
That wonderful Christmas night.

Chorus:
Jesus came down to earth on Christmas.
Yes, our Savior came Christmas night;
The angels sang of His glory,
The sky filled with God's great light.

HUMBLE BIRTH

by Helen Kitchell Evans
Sung to: Twinkle, Twinkle, Little Star

Just a little bed of hay,
For my Lord on Christmas day,
No nice pillow for His head,
No soft covers on His bed,
Yet this babe of humble birth
Came to save all on this earth.

SS1868

CHRISTMAS PLAYS

ON STAGE!

by Helen Kitchell Evans
Dramatic Interpretation

Dramatic interpretation is a way of learning through various kinds of dramatic situations. The children are helped to deepen their concepts by active, creative participation in a wide variety of experiences.

Kindergarten and primary school children need challenging materials so they can learn to fully converse. Upper grades need provision for materials that will enable them to have more finished productions.

Teachers, who do dramatics, need to be scavengers, collecting boxes, empty spools, broom handles, jewelry, purses, old clothes, etc. All of these are potential costumes and stage properties.

Situations that arise in the various areas of the curriculum are filled with opportunity for dramatization.

First, there is dramatic play where the children dramatize a trip they have made to the post office, the firehouse or library. This type of play gives the teacher an excellent opportunity to observe the behavior of her children.

Second is the playwriting where the children develop their own lines and present their own plays.

Third, the use of puppets often helps reveal many social and emotional problems. It is often easier for a child to stand behind a puppet stage and speak through the puppet. Many children will participate in this manner when they refuse to stand before a class.

Fourth, is the use of the printed play which is the culmination of all the other learning processes. Plays, such as those on pages 53-74, offer this type of training for the children.

To present this type of play the following instructions may be helpful:

1. Begin by reading the play to the children.
2. Be very sure that they understand the meaning of all words and have some idea of the background of the characters.
3. Re-read the play asking various children to repeat the lines (if they cannot read) and for readers have them read various parts as you continue through the play.
4. Listen for their interpretation of certain characters before selecting the cast. If the play is being done solely for the joy of reading, a cast need not be selected. However, if being presented for the public the best should be chosen. There will be some disappointment but that, too, is a part of learning. All are not super in everything.
5. When parts have been selected then children must memorize before rehearsal. Do not tire the children with long rehearsal periods. Better shorter periods over a longer time. We want dramatization to be a joy not a task! Don't be afraid to try! HAPPY CASTING!

SS1868

THE WONDROUS BIRTH

by Edith E. Cutting

Cast of Characters

Narrator
Innkeeper
Innkeeper's wife
Innkeeper's son
Mary
Joseph

4 shepherds
1 angel who announces the birth
Other angels who join the first
3 wise men

Presentation

The narrator stands at one side of the stage with the light only on him as he reads the introduction to each scene. When he stops reading, that light goes out, and the lights come up on the scene itself. At the end of the scene, the lights go out and the narrator's light comes on again.

Narrator: Each year we rejoice at this time, in the wondrous story of the birth of Jesus, the Son of God. Let us hear first how St. Luke begins the story.

And it came to pass in those days, that there went out a decree from Caesar Augustus, that all the world should be taxed . . . And all went to be taxed, everyone into his own city. And Joseph also went up from Galilee, out of the city of Nazareth, into Judaea, unto the city of David, which is called Bethlehem; (because he was of the house and lineage of David:) to be taxed with Mary his espoused wife, being great with child. Luke 2:1, 3-5

SS1868

Scene I

(Kitchen of an inn in Bethlehem. The innkeeper's wife is stirring a big kettle over the fire as her husband brings in a bucket of charcoal.)

Innkeeper: Well, business is certainly good this year. Caesar Augustus did us a favor for once, sending everybody back to their hometowns to be registered. We haven't had this many people in Bethlehem in years.

Wife: I know. The big room is already crowded, and the smaller ones are all taken.

Innkeeper: I should say they are. I just agreed to let a man have our room for his family. We'll have to sleep here by the fire tonight.

Innkeeper's son: *(Comes running in.)* Father, there's a man and his wife who want lodging for the night.

Innkeeper: Too bad. There isn't a bit of space left.

Wife: Tell them to try farther down the street. Maybe Jacob has some room.

Son: He says he's tried everywhere, and his wife needs a place—

Innkeeper: Everybody needs a place, but there isn't a cubit left here. They'll have to sleep in the streets like a lot of other people.

Son: But the lady is going to have a baby.

Wife: A baby! Well, she can't be left out on the street for that. She'd be better off in the stable than out there.

Innkeeper: But the stable's full, too.

Son: I could fasten my little donkey out back, and they could have that stall.

Innkeeper: You've never wanted me to let out that stall since I gave you the donkey.

Son: I know, Father, but this is different. The lady looks so tired. I would put clean straw in, and I'm sure she wouldn't mind.

Wife: I'll go out and see what she says. At least they would be by themselves instead of crowded in with all the others.

(She leaves with her son, and the husband pokes up the fire, shaking his head.)

Narrator: And so it was, that, while they were there, the days were accomplished that she should be delivered. And she brought forth her firstborn son, and wrapped him in swaddling clothes, and laid him in a manger because there was no room for them in the inn. Luke 2:6-7

Scene II

(Stable of the inn. The boy is bringing in armfuls of fresh straw. He puts some in the manger and some on the floor beside it. His mother comes in with Mary and Joseph.)

Innkeeper's wife: It's the best we can do. My husband has even let one family have our own room, but you will be by yourselves here—better than crowded into the big room with everybody else.

Innkeeper: *(Calls from offstage.)* Wife!

Mary: Yes, this is clean and quiet. It's good of you to take us in at all.

Wife: It was my son who thought of it. But you will be warm here.

Innkeeper: Wife!

Wife: I have to go now. We're so busy tonight. But if you need me, your husband can call. *(She bustles out.)*

Boy: Do you have blankets? I could bring my little donkey's saddle blanket.

Joseph: Thank you, but we do have blankets. *(He starts to open a bundle.)* We'll spread this for my wife. *(Boy helps him spread it over the straw on the floor.)* And here is a smaller one my wife made. *(He spreads that over the straw in the manger.)*

Boy: I'll go now, but if you want anything, just shout for me, and I'll come running. I'm going to be an innkeeper like my father when I grow up, so I like to practice.

Mary: Thank you, little innkeeper. I'm sure you will be a good one. Good night, now.

Boy: *(As he leaves.)* Good night.

Narrator: And there were in the same country shepherds abiding in the field, keeping watch over their flock by night. And, lo, the angel of the Lord came upon them, and the glory of the Lord shone round about them: and they were sore afraid. Luke 2:8-9

Scene III

In the field two shepherds are sleeping and two keeping watch. All is quiet till a sound of singing begins softly offstage: "It Came Upon the Midnight Clear," or "While Shepherds Watched Their Flocks." The two sleepers sit up, and as the light becomes bright (Spotlight.), they throw their arms up to cover their faces. The angel comes out into the light.

Angel: . . . Fear not: for, behold, I bring you good tidings of great joy, which shall be to all people. For unto you is born this day in the city of David, a Saviour which is Christ the Lord. And this shall be a sign unto you: Ye shall find the babe wrapped in swaddling clothes, lying in a manger. Luke 2:10-12

Other Angels: *(Quickly appearing and surrounding the first to say in unison.)* Glory to God in the highest, and on earth peace, good will toward men. Luke 2:14

(The light fades, and the angels disappear backstage, repeating more softly: Glory to God in the highest . . . .)

1st Shepherd: Did you see? Did you hear what I did?

2nd Shepherd: I think I was dreaming.

3rd Shepherd: We could not all have dreamed the same thing, if we truly heard it, let us say it together.

4th Shepherd: Yes, that's right. If you heard the same thing as I, tell it with me. I was scared, but the first thing the angel said was, "Fear not . . . "

4th and 1st: For behold, I bring you good tidings of great joy,

3rd joins in: Which shall be to all people.

2nd joins: For unto you is born this day in the city of David, a Saviour which is Christ the Lord—

1st Shepherd: *(Interrupting.)* But the city of David is Bethlehem! *(Points.)* That is just over there.

2nd, 3rd, 4th: *(Continue in unison.)* And this shall be a sign unto you: Ye shall find the babe wrapped in swaddling clothes, lying in a manger.

2nd Shepherd: And then they all praised God together.

3rd Shepherd: *(Stands.)* Then let us go. Come on. The angel meant us to go. He said, "Ye shall find the babe . . . ."

1st Shepherd: *(Stands.)* Yes, we can go to Bethlehem and be back before sunrise.

4th Shepherd: But we can't all go and leave the sheep. I will stay. I have seen glory such as I never expected to in this life. You younger men go. You can go faster, and I will stay with the sheep.

1st Shepherd: You are right, Father. Someone must stay. We will hurry back to tell you what we have seen.

2nd Shepherd: Can what we see be greater than what we have already seen?

3rd Shepherd: Yes, it will be, for surely angels are not as great as the Lord whom they announce. Come, let us go even unto Bethlehem.

(All but one hurry out; he settles himself to wait.)

Narrator: And it came to pass, as the angels were gone away from them into heaven, the shepherds said one to another, Let us now go even unto Bethlehem, and see this thing which is come to pass, which the Lord had made known unto us. And they came with haste, and found Mary, and Joseph, and the babe lying in a manger. Luke 2:15-16

Scene IV

(The stable. Mary finishes wrapping the baby in swaddling clothes and hands him to Joseph.)

Mary: And his name shall be Jesus. Oh, Joseph, he is so beautiful!

Joseph: Yes. *(He lays the baby in the manger.)* There, little Jesus, are you comfortable? *(He turns to Mary.)* He is beautiful, indeed. Now you must rest.

(There is a knock; then a man in rough clothing peers into the stall. He comes in, followed by two others. Joseph moves to stand in front of Mary, but the three men kneel.)

Joseph: Who are you? What are you doing here?

1st Shepherd: We are shepherds from the fields beyond the city.

2nd Shepherd: We come not to disturb you but to see the baby, which is Christ the Lord.

3rd Shepherd: An angel appeared to us. He said we should go unto the city of David and we would find the baby wrapped in swaddling clothes.

 SS1868

Mary: You were told this?

1st Shepherd: Yes, and the angel told us not to be afraid.

2nd Shepherd: We were scared at first. The light was so great.

3rd Shepherd: But he said he brought good tidings for all people.

Mary: Joseph, they were told, even as we were.

Joseph: Yes. What else did the angel say?

1st Shepherd: "Glory to God in the highest—"

2nd Shepherd: There were other angels that came, and they all said together, "Glory to God in the highest . . . ."

3rd Shepherd: "And on earth peace," they said, "peace and good will to men."

1st Shepherd: And we have seen as he said we would, a baby in swaddling clothes. *(Stands.)* We will leave you now to rest. We must go back to our sheep.

2nd Shepherd: *(Stands.)* But we will always remember.

3rd Shepherd: And we will tell our families and everyone we meet. (Stands.)

1st Shepherd: For we are blessed to have seen the Savior, which is Christ the Lord, when He first came to earth.

(They bow and leave, and Joseph closes the door behind them.)

Narrator: And when they had seen it, they made known abroad the saying which was told them concerning this child. And all they that heard it wondered at those things which were told them by the shepherds. But Mary kept all these things, and pondered them in her heart. Luke 2:17-19

Listen further, as St. Matthew also tells us of that wondrous time:

Now when Jesus was born in Bethlehem of Judaea in the days of Herod the king, behold, there came wise men from the east to Jerusalem, Saying, "Where is he that is born King of the Jews? for we have seen his star in the east, and are come to worship him." Matthew 2:1-2

SS1868

Scene V

(Three wise men stand outside Jerusalem palace after having visited Herod the king.)

1st Wise man: Surely this is not the king we seek.

2nd Wise man: No, nor the place. See, the star goes on ahead. We are not there yet.

3rd Wise man: I thought, of course, Jerusalem would be the place. It has been the great city of Israel for a thousand years. Yet King Herod seemed troubled when we asked where the King of the Jews was born.

1st Wise man: But surely the scribes he called about him must be right. They would have studied the Scriptures to know about this great coming.

2nd Wise man: Yes, and they said the king would be born in Bethlehem, not Jerusalem, but they did not know he had already been born.

3rd Wise man: Sometimes I wonder. Perhaps we are wrong.

1st Wise man: You cannot think that. We have been sure of the great star we followed, and it has brought us this far.

2nd Wise man: Yes, through deserts and over mountains and across rivers.

3rd Wise man: You are right. We have been blessed to have seen His star, and soon we shall see the king himself. *(All leave.)*

Narrator: When they had heard the king, they departed; and, lo, the star, which they saw in the east, went before them, till it came and stood over where the young child was. When they saw the star, they rejoiced with exceeding great joy. And when they were come into the house, they saw the young child with Mary his mother, and fell down, and worshipped him: and when they had opened their treasures, they presented unto him gifts; gold, and frankincense, and myrrh. Matthew 2:9-11

Scene VI

(Room in small house. Joseph stands beside Mary, who sits on the floor or small stool. The child lies on a blanket near her.)

Mary: It will soon be time to present the child in the temple.

Joseph: Yes, the days go by quickly. I have found carpentry work enough to pay for our lodging in this small house as long as we need to stay, and I have registered with the Roman authorities. Now we must think of the future.

(There is a knock on the door. Joseph opens it, then steps back as he sees three richly dressed men there.)

Joseph: Sires, will you come in? We are only humble people here. *(They enter.)*

1st Wise man: Thank you for your courtesy. We come in peace, searching for the newborn King of the Jews.

2nd Wise man: We followed his star from the East. It has stopped here in Bethlehem, and this must be the child.

3rd Wise man: Let us kneel as we approach the king. *(They kneel, and Joseph also.)*

1st Wise man: I have brought gold for him, a gift fit for a king. *(He opens his purse and pours gold coins onto the floor.)* May his life be a rich gift, of great value to all people.

2nd Wise man: Frankincense, strong and fragrant, have I brought for the newborn king. *(He lays a leather sack on the floor.)* It is meet that this gift comes from the Far East, for this child will be king of the whole world.

3rd Wise man: And I bring myrrh. *(He also lays a pouch beside the child.)* It is bitter, indeed, for no one's life is only of sweetness. This child's life will have bitterness and pain, but from it will come strength for others who suffer.

(Slowly the men rise to their feet.)

Joseph: We thank you for these gifts for the babe. We will treasure them for his use.

1st Wise man: And so we take our leave, to return to the east whence we came.

2nd Wise man: May God bless you and the child.

3rd wise man: And may the star lead others as it has led us to him.

(They leave, and Joseph closes the door.)

Narrator: And being warned of God in a dream that they should not return to Herod, they departed into their own country another way. Matthew 2:12

So ends the story of the wondrous coming of Jesus, but the whole story does not end there. There is much, much more. It has been told and retold through all the years since then. The shepherds told their children, and the wise men told other wise men, and I—I am the son, a hundred generations removed, of the boy who made room for the Holy Child in his father's stable. So the story never ends, but lives and moves in our hearts and our children's hearts forever!

SS1868

A DIFFERENT NIGHT BEFORE CHRISTMAS

by Patty Medill

CAST:

Narrator   Wife

Man   Children (two or more)

OPTIONAL CAST:

Christ, Angels, Mary, Joseph, Shepherds, Wisemen, Animals, Choir, etc.

Play should be read by Narrator as cast pantomimes.

Act I
Scene I

(Bedroom with window, fireplace with Bible on mantle, and table with lamp—man, in old fashioned nightshirt, and wife asleep in bed(s).

'Twas the night before Christmas, and all through the house,

Not a creature was stirring, not even a mouse.

The Bible was laid on the mantle with care,

No thought that soon, perhaps Christ would be there.

The children had wandered off to their own beds,

No thought of eternity entered their heads;

And Mama in her kerchief and I in my cap,

Had just settled down for a long winter's nap.

When out on the lawn there arose such a clatter,

I sprang from my bed to see what was the matter. *(Man sits up in bed, startled.)*

Away to the window I flew like a flash,

Tore open the shutters and threw up the sash. *(Man hurries to window and opens curtains.)*

The moon on the breast of the new fallen snow

Gave a luster of midday to objects below.

When what to my wondering eyes should appear,

But a man clothed in white, with a band to the rear.

(Optional—Jesus and angels appear outside of window.)

The band was of angels who worshipped the King,

The trumpet was sounded, they started to sing.

The man looked right at me and called me by name,

"What's been done with your life?" I bowed down in shame.

(Man bows down before Jesus. Jesus can shake a finger at the man during quoted parts. Man can shake his head "no" as the following questions are asked.)

"Helped the sick? Fed the hungry? Told people of me?"

Why, I can't even account for my own family.

"Have you taken your children to church faithfully,
Have you told them the story of Calvary?
"Have you taught them about my birth in a stall,
Do they know any story about me at all?"

(Jesus and the angels leave, and the man returns to his bed. To make the first part seem like a dream, several things can be done. It could be acted out as a shadow play with sheets between the audience and the actors, a thin filmy material could be used as a curtain, or dry ice could be used to create a cloudy effect. If any are used, they should be removed at this point.)

I turned from my sleep and I opened my eyes,
It was with great relief that I then realized,
All that had happened, as real as it seemed,
Had not really happened, it was only a dream!
I rose from my bed and turned on the light.
I knelt down to pray and consider my plight.

(Man rises, turns on lamp, and kneels to pray.)

I gathered the children, my wife, and myself,
Then took the old Bible down from the shelf.

(Narrator will need to pause to give the man time to pray, gather his wife and children, and get the Bible from the mantle.)

They all sat and stared with a strange puzzled look.
I smiled and explained as I opened the book,
Tomorrow is Christmas, we thought we were set,
But the *true* story of Christmas we've seemed to forget.

(The man acts as though he is going to read the Christmas story.)

Act I
Scene II (Optional)

If possible, have the manger scene set up in a different place. All lights go off and the manger is spotlighted as the narrator reads the Christmas story from Luke 2:1-20. The play is very flexible here. Shepherds in the field may be added, with angels to proclaim the birth. Wise men may be added if Matthew 2:1 and 2 is read. If a choir is to be used, they can sing songs such as "Away in a Manger," "Silent Night," "Hark the Herald Angels Sing," "Joy to the World," "We Three Kings," etc. at the proper intervals as the Scripture is being read. If there are a lot of children, they can be used as animals around the manger, etc.)

Act I
Scene III

(Same setting as Scene I—Family has remained to hear the Bible story.)
As I finished the story we all understood,
The feeling between us was loving and good.
The true purpose of Christmas is not of this earth,
But through giving and love we recall the birth,
Of the gift that the Father gave us that day, knowing that
Through His Son the world would be saved.
We can happily say as we turn out the light,
(Lights on all play participants.)
All play participants in unison:
   MERRY CHRISTMAS TO ALL AND TO ALL A GOODNIGHT!

BIG NEWS IN BETHLEHEM

by Helen Kitchell Evans

Cast of Characters: John
                             David

Setting: Anywhere in Bethlehem some time after Jesus' birth.

(As scene opens the two boys are excitedly talking.)

John: David, did you hear about what happened in our town?

David: Yes, everyone in Bethlehem is talking about it. That is a very special baby that was born.

John: He was born in a manger. They say that all the inns were filled.

David: I know. Mother says that it's terrible trying to find a place to stay. It's so crowded in Bethlehem when all the people arrive to pay their taxes. It's like this every tax season.

John: I heard that an angel came to some shepherds out in a field not far away. I wonder if those shepherds were scared.

David: I don't know, but I tell you for sure that I would have been. Who ever saw an angel?

SS1868

John:	I believe that they were not afraid. The first thing the angel said was, "Don't be afraid."
David:	After that other angels came and sang, GLORY TO GOD IN THE HIGHEST, PEACE ON EARTH AND GOOD WILL TOWARD MEN.
John:	They did? How did you hear that?
David:	Mother told me about it.
John:	Just imagine being born on a pile of dirty hay. Poor little baby!
David:	Hay isn't always dirty, John. I took a nap on a pile of hay on my grandfather's farm. It's sweet and smells fresh. Not really bad at all.
John:	Also, we heard that three wise men from the east came to see him. They brought with them frankincense, myrrh and gold.
David:	I know what gold is, but what is that other stuff?
John:	I don't know either, but Mother says it is very good incense and perfume. It costs a lot, too.
David:	This will be a time that Bethlethem will never forget. They say he has been named Jesus.
John:	He is to be the Savior of the world.
David:	I can't see how a baby can save the world.
John:	Well, God, the Father, will take care of all things in His time. I'd better go home, let me know if you hear any other news about Jesus.
David:	Isn't it wonderful that this happened in this little town of Bethlehem? See you later, John.

(They part, each going in a different direction.)

SS1868

NO ROOM IN THE INN

by Marilyn Senterfitt

Cast of Characters: Sarah
Mother
Father
Joseph
Narrator

Ten or more children may participate in this play. Nonspeaking parts include Mary and guests in the inn. Shepherds may be added and other children may be animals in the stable. See suggestions for scenery, props and costumes on page 90-93.

(Narrator stands at stage left. In the stable, animals are alseep. In the inn, the guests are seated at the tables, and Father and Mother are waiting on them.)

Narrator: This was going to be a night of nights. It was made for miracles. This is the story of one of those miracles.

(Mother picks up bread and cheese.)

Mother: Sarah, come carry this food to the far table. That family has just arrived from Jerusalem.

(Sarah enters stage right, moving slowly toward her mother. She leans on her crutch.)

Narrator: Sarah had been crippled from birth. She enjoyed helping her parents in the inn and didn't mind when strangers whispered about her foot. It was a part of her and she had long ago accepted it.

(Sarah takes the food from her mother.)

Sarah: How I wish that we could go to Jerusalem and see the temple. I've never been past the hills outside of Bethlehem.

(Father walks up.)

Father: I, for one, am glad not to have to travel a long distance to be taxed like all these people. For once it is a blessing to have been born in Bethlehem and to have lived here all my life!

(Sarah takes the food to the table and returns to her mother.)

Mother: Child, you better go to bed. It is very late. Your father and I can manage now.

Sarah: I am very tired, I'll be up early to help with the morning meal. Good night.

Mother: Good night. Sleep well.

Father: Good night, Sarah.

(Sarah moves toward her pallet.)

Father: I want to cry when I see how she has to lean on that crutch.

Mother: She is such a good child. We have reason to praise God, but I wish she were whole like other children.

SS1868

Narrator: Sarah was so weary. It has been a long day. She was glad to finally sleep.

(Sarah puts her crutch aside and lies down. She looks out at the bright star.)

Sarah: What a beautiful star! It seems to be right over the inn. The courtyard is as bright as day!

(Sarah yawns and stretches and is soon asleep. Guests leave stage right. Mother and Father clean up and Mother exits stage right, also.)

Narrator: Not all travelers had found a comfortable bed on this night. Sarah's father had late callers.

(Mary and Joseph enter stage right and go to center front of inn. Mary leans on Joseph as he knocks on the door. Father comes to the door.)

Father: Yes, yes. What do you want?

Joseph: Sir, we have traveled far. My wife is very weary and the child will be born soon. We seek a room.

(Sarah wakes. She sits up and listens.)

Father: I am truly sorry, but the inn is full. I haven't a bed or corner left.

Joseph: Please, sir. You cannot turn us away. I don't ask for myself, but for my wife.

(Father shakes head and turns away. Sarah stretches as if she were trying to look out a window.)

Sarah: How weary she looks. I must give her my bed.

(Sarah struggles to her feet. Mary and Joseph start to leave as Father moves back to the door.)

Father: Wait! There is the stable. At least you will have a roof over your head.

Joseph: God bless you, sir.

Narrator: Sarah's father showed the man and woman to the stable. Father wished he had another room so they could be more comfortable. He felt sorry for the woman.

(Father returns to the inn. Sarah is waiting at the door.)

Father: Sarah, what are you doing up?

Sarah: I heard voices, Father.

Father: It was two travelers from Nazareth. I put them in the stable. It will be warm and dry there. Now off to bed with you.

(Sarah goes to bed and lies down but she only tosses and turns. In the stable Mary places the doll in the manger. Soon the shepherds enter quietly and kneel at the manger.)

Narrator: In the stable the miracle of miracles happened. A promised baby was born. Soon the Good News was shared with lowly shepherds who came to worship the newborn babe. In the inn, Sarah was unable to sleep.

(Sarah sits up.)

Sarah: I can't get them off my mind. They must be hungry. I'll take them some food.

(Sarah gathers up bread, cheese and a pitcher. The shepherds exit stage left before she moves across the courtyard toward the stable. She shyly approaches the manger and hands the food to Joseph. She then looks down at the manger.)

Sarah: Oh! What a beautiful baby. Is it a boy?

(Mary nods her head. She and Joseph smile broadly. Sarah places her crutch on the ground and kneels by the manger. She touches the baby and smiles. She soon rises.)

Sarah: I must go, but I will be back in the morning and will bring you more food.

(Sarah moves out into the courtyard. The crutch remains in in the stable and she no longer limps. Sarah looks back at the stable.)

Sarah: What a beautiful baby. I don't understand it, but I feel such a deep love for Him.

(Sarah goes to the center of the courtyard. Her parents enter from stage right through the inn door and hurry toward her.)

Mother: Where have you been? I went to check on you and I was afraid something had happened to you.

Father: Sarah, where is your crutch?

(Sarah looks down and in that moment realizes she no longer needs her crutch. Her once crippled foot is now whole and strong. She begins to jump, run and whirl around the courtyard, laughing aloud. The guests enter stage right and stare. Sarah goes to her parents and they embrace.)

Mother: What has happened, Sarah?

Father: Yes, my child. What happened to cause this great miracle?

(Sarah looks toward the stable.)

Sarah: The babe is born! The babe is born!

(Sarah and her parents move to the stable and kneel at the manger. The guests quietly follow and gather around the manger. When all are in place the narrator speaks.)

Narrator: This has been Sarah's story. Some may claim it is only a legend, but who can truly say? It was a wondrous night made for miracles, and the greatest of these was the miracle of God's Son, Jesus Christ, being born in a stable in Bethlehem because there was no room in the inn.

Shining Star Publications, Copyright © 1988, A Division of Good Apple, Inc.   SS1868

THE SHEPHERD WHO WAS LEFT BEHIND

by Marilyn Senterfitt

PREPARATION

PROPS: Nativity scene—manger filled with straw, two chairs, a large cloth, doll, small blanket, cheese, bread and fruit. A large star made from yellow poster board and gold glitter may be placed over scene. Shepherds will need sticks for crooks. Sheep can be made from white poster paper. A little greenery will add to the outdoor feeling. Large clouds can be constructed from white poster board or tissue paper attached to two sturdy frames or partitions.

SETTING THE SCENE: On stage right place the manger, two chairs covered with cloth and the doll and blanket hidden behind chairs. On stage left set up two large clouds with center opening through which angels appear. Provide chairs for angels to sit in behind the clouds when not on stage. Place two chairs or benches in front of clouds and cover with brown or green cloth. The shepherds will stand or sit around these. Place greenery around the seats and attach two or three sheep to the cloth.

SPEAKING PARTS: Samuel, Joel, Aaron, Gabriel, all angels, and the narrator.

NON-SPEAKING PARTS: Mary, Joseph, innkeeper, other shepherds.

 SS1868

(Innkeeper is sitting or standing near Nativity scene. Mary and Joseph are in rear of room. Narrator stands stage left. Unrolls scroll and begins. Mary and Joseph start slowly toward front.)

NARRATOR: And it came to pass in those days there went out a decree from Caesar Augustus, that all the world should be taxed. And this taxing was first made when Cyrenius was governor of Syria. And all went to be taxed, every one into his own city. And Joseph also went up from Galilee, out of the city of Nazareth, into Judaea, unto the city of David: to be taxed with Mary his espoused wife, being great with child.

(Before narrator finishes reading the above, Mary and Joseph arrive at front. Pretend to knock on door. Innkeeper shakes head. They reluctantly turn away. Innkeeper takes Joseph's arm and leads them to stable. Mary and Joseph need to be settled before baby is born.)

NARRATOR: And so it was, that, while they were there, the days were accomplished that she should be delivered.

(Mary brings out doll, wraps in blanket and places in manger.)

NARRATOR: And she brought forth her firstborn son, and wrapped him in swaddling clothes, and laid him in a manger; because there was no room for them in the inn.

(Shepherds enter stage left and gather around cloth covered chairs. Some sit down. May say a few "bah-bahs" for effect. As the narration continues Mary and Joseph care for the baby. Innkeeper brings cheese, bread and fruit, kneels by manger and admires baby. Mary, Joseph and innkeeper stay in character and should not watch the shepherds or audience.)

NARRATOR: And there were in the same country shepherds abiding in the field, keeping watch over their flocks by night. And, lo, the angel of the Lord came upon them, and the glory of the Lord shone round them: and they were sore afraid.

(Gabriel appears to shepherds from behind cloud stage left. Shepherds show fright. Hide their eyes but when angel speaks they listen intently.)

NARRATOR: And the angel said unto them,
(Gabriel holds out arms.)

GABRIEL: Fear not: for, behold, I bring you good tidings of great joy, which shall be to all people. For unto you is born this day in the city of David a Saviour, which is Christ the Lord. And this shall be a sign unto you; Ye shall find the babe wrapped in swaddling clothes, lying in a manger.

(Other angels appear from behind clouds, lining up to left and right of Gabriel.)

NARRATOR: And suddenly there was with the angel a multitude of the heavenly host praising God, and saying,

ANGELS: Glory to God in the highest, and on earth peace, good will toward men.

(Angels move quietly back behind clouds.)

NARRATOR: And it came to pass, as the angels were gone away from them, the shepherds said one to another:

AARON: Let us now go even unto Bethlehem, and see this thing which the Lord hath made known unto us.

(All shepherds begin to move toward stable. Aaron motions for Samuel to remain behind. Samuel kicks ground with disappointment. Other shepherds come to manger and kneel there as play continues.)

NARRATOR: And they came with haste, and found the baby lying in a manger and Mary and Joseph.

(Joel peeks out from cloud stage right. Samuel sits with head in hands looking unhappy.)

NARRATOR: As the shepherds hurry to Bethlehem, a young angel is interested in the plight of Samuel, the shepherd who was left behind.

JOEL: He looks so sad. I wonder if I could go down and maybe cheer him up a little? Gabriel, may I ask a question?

(Gabriel sticks head out from behind cloud stage left.)

GABRIEL: Yes, Joel, what do you want? I'm very busy. Everything is happening so fast tonight?

JOEL: Sir, may I go down and see the boy who was left behind to watch the sheep? He looks so unhappy.

(Gabriel looks down at Samuel.)

GABRIEL: I don't know, Joel. We were only supposed to appear to announce the baby's birth.

JOEL: Please, Gabriel, I'll only stay a little while.

SS1868

GABRIEL: I suppose it wouldn't do any harm. He does look miserable. Yes, you have permission.

JOEL: Thank you, sir!

(Joel steps out in full view of Samuel.)

SAMUEL: Another angel! I can't take all this appearing and disappearing! What do you want?

(Joel sits down with Samuel.)

JOEL: I'm Joel and just wanted to keep you company. I used to be a shepherd.

SAMUEL: My name is Samuel. You mean you were a shepherd before you . . . .

JOEL: You can say it! Before I died I was a shepherd like you. I helped my father tend one hundred sheep outside Bethany. I liked it very much.

SAMUEL: Do you like being an angel?

JOEL: It's different but really exciting. Everyone is talking about tonight. God has been planning this for a very long time.

SAMUEL: Does that mean Aaron and the others will really find the Savior down in Bethlehem?

JOEL: Of course they will! Angels don't lie!

SAMUEL: I didn't mean to hurt your feelings. It's just all so hard to believe.

JOEL: Didn't you learn in synagogue that God would someday send a Messiah?

SAMUEL: Yes, but I thought he would come in a golden chariot and have a great army to defeat all our enemies.

JOEL: He could have done that! Gabriel, he's the one who spoke to you awhile ago, says God wanted His Son to come to earth just like we did, as a tiny baby.

SAMUEL: But what can a little baby do?

JOEL: I guess it would be all right to tell you some of the things He's going to do when He grows up.

SAMUEL: What are they?

(Joel takes a deep breath and speaks rapidly.)

JOEL: Gabriel says He is going to heal blind people, help the lame to walk, cast out demons, walk on water and raise the dead!

SAMUEL: All that?

JOEL: And much, much more. Then Gabriel said at the chosen time He will have to die on a cross.

SAMUEL: What! Someone is going to do that to God's Son? That's terrible!

JOEL: Yes, but God planned it that way.

SAMUEL: Why would God let anyone hurt His Son?

JOEL: Because He loves you.

SAMUEL: God loves me?

Shining Star Publications, Copyright © 1988, A Division of Good Apple, Inc. SS1868

JOEL: Yes, that's why Jesus is here. By the way, Jesus is the baby's name. You see God hates sin and all the people on earth are sinners, but He loves them and He has sent Jesus to show them a way to be forgiven.

SAMUEL: But what do we have to do?

JOEL: You ~~just~~ have to believe in Jesus and ask God to forgive you.

SAMUEL: And Jesus has to die so that I can be forgiven?

JOEL: Yes, but He will come back to life.

SAMUEL: Joel, nobody can do that!

JOEL: God's Son can!

SAMUEL: Are you sure angels never tell lies?

JOEL: Never!

SAMUEL: Then all the things you've told me are really true?

JOEL: On my honor as a former shepherd—and angel in good standing. It is all true.

SAMUEL: I've never heard anything so wonderful!

(The other shepherds start back from Bethlehem.)

JOEL: I must go, Samuel. I am only allowed to speak to you. Good-bye!

SAMUEL: Good-bye, Joel. Thank you for keeping me company!

(Joel moves behind cloud. Aaron hurries to Samuel. He and the other shepherds are very excited.)

AARON: Samuel, it was just as the angel said! The baby was there in the manger. You've got to see Him. Joshua will show you the way. It's all so wonderful!

(Samuel moves toward Bethlehem with Joshua. He pauses at center stage and smiling broadly speaks to the audience.)

SAMUEL: Yes, and it's just the beginning!

(All the angels and shepherds move to the stable scene.)

NARRATOR: The Bible says, "For God so loved the world, that he gave his only begotten Son, that whosoever believeth in him should not perish, but have everlasting life." This is the true meaning of Christmas. Won't you join us now as we sing together "Joy to the World" and thank God for the wonderful gift of His Son, Jesus Christ.

(After the carol is sung, the play ends as Mary, holding the baby, and Joseph walk to rear followed by the innkeeper, shepherds and angels. The narrator rolls up scroll and follows angels. Christmas carols can be played softly as performers file out. As narrator leaves stage the volume of the music can increase.)

THE END

Shining Star Publications, Copyright © 1988, A Division of Good Apple, Inc. SS1868

MAHLI'S SHEEPSKIN JACKET

by Edith E. Cutting

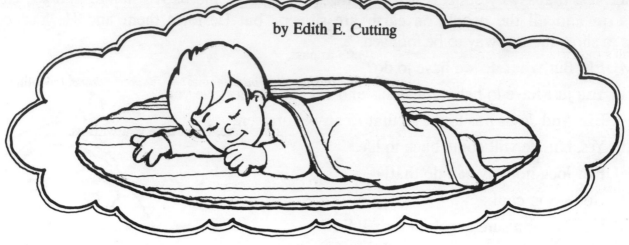

Cast of Characters

Mahli (Mah-li)	His father	Mary
His mother	Other shepherds	Joseph

Scenery

The stage settings should be very bare and simple, to encourage imagination and to make changing easy.

Scene I

(A shepherd's home. Mahli is asleep on a pad on the floor. His mother is shaking him gently by the shoulder.)

Mother: Mahli, wake up. Mahli!

Mahli: *(Sits up.)* Yes, mother. *(Flops, back to sleep again.)*

Mother: Wake up, Mahli. *(Shakes him again.)* You must go out where the sheep are and see if your father is all right.

Mahli: *(Sits up again and rubs eyes.)* What's the matter, Mother? What happened?

Mother: There's a strange light in the sky near that big star. And the sound of singing.

Mahli: Singing! The shepherds don't sing.

Mother: I know. It might be angels, but who knows? Oh, Mahli, hurry. I'm worried about your father.

Mahli: *(Gets up.)* Can I wear my new sheepskin jacket?

Mother: Of course. *(She begins wrapping bread and cheese in a cloth.)* So you like your new jacket?

Mahli: Oh, Mother, it's beautiful. It's just like Father's. And I have wanted one for such a long time.

Mother: I know you have, dear. I meant to get it made sooner, but I had to make things for your new baby brother. And then there was the baby next door. And Aunt Susan's baby.

Mahli: *(Smooths his hand down the jacket.)* It is just as soft as the baby's skin.

Mother: Good. I hope it will keep you warm for a long time. *(Hands him the bundle.)* Now take this food to your father, and then run back and tell me what has happened.

(Mahli hurries out. Stage is darkened.)

SS1868

Scene II

(The shepherds' field. The men are all standing in one corner and talking, when Mahli comes running in.)

Mahli's father: Let us go and see what has come to pass.

Mahli: What has come to pass, Father? *(He pushes the bundle into his father's hand.)* Mother sent this—

Father: Yes, yes, but there is no time to eat now. Since you are here, I will take you with us.

Mahli: Where are we going?

1st Shepherd: To Bethlehem to see the babe the angels told us about.

2nd Shepherd: It isn't far.

3rd Shepherd: But we can't all go and leave the sheep alone.

1st Shepherd: It won't take us long.

3rd Shepherd: Too long to leave the flocks alone. Suppose something else happened and frightened them?

2nd Shepherd: The angels didn't frighten them.

Mahli's father: We have wondered about the big star for a long time. It must be a sign of the Savior. Now the angels have told us where to find Him, I think we should go.

3rd Shepherd: I've heard and seen the angels. I shall remember all my life. You go, and I will stay with the sheep.

Mahli's father: *(Puts bundle down by him.)* Come, then, let us start. If we hurry, we can be back before dawn.

(The shepherds cross the stage as lights go out. They come down from the stage and cross in front of it on their way to Bethlehem, talking all the time.)

Mahli: Mother said I should come back and tell her if you were all right.

Father: You will have more to tell her than that. Angels spoke to us this night—angels from heaven— and they said the Messiah is born.

Mahli: The Messiah?

Father: Yes, the promised Savior. We shall see Him. You shall see Him, and remember Him all your days.

Mahli: Will He be like a king?

Father: No, there's no palace in Bethlehem. But He will be special. You shall tell your children of this night, and your children's children.

Scene III

(The manger scene. As the lights go up, the shepherds appear on the far side of the stage. The star is shining above an open stable on the other side. Mary is seated beside a manger, and Joseph is standing near her.)

Mahli: But this is just a stable.

Father: Hush. See the star? *(They all come closer. The older shepherds kneel, but Mahli stays standing to look over their heads.)*

1st Shepherd: We have come to see the baby that is to be the Savior.

Joseph: We welcome you.

2nd Shepherd: Angels came to us in the field. They said not to be afraid. They said they had tidings of great joy.

Mahli's father: Good tidings for all people.

1st Shepherd: They said to go to Bethlehem, and we would find a baby wrapped in swaddling clothes and lying in a manger. It's just the way they said.

2nd Shepherd: Then they all said, "Glory to God in the Highest—"

Mahli's father: "And on earth, peace, good will toward men."

1st Shepherd: It was like music.

(While the men have been explaining, Mahli has stood quietly, looking at the baby and running his hand up and down his jacket. Now the men stand up.)

Mahli's father: We must go back now. Come, Mahli.

(As the men go out, Mahli hurries to the manger. He pulls off his jacket and lays it in Mary's lap.)

Mahli: It's too big for the baby now, but it would be soft for him to lie on. *(He touches the baby's cheek, then turns back to Mary.)* My mother made the jacket. It's like the grown-up shepherds wear.

Mary: It's beautiful, but your mother may not want you to give it away. She must have worked hard to make it so soft and warm.

Mahli: *(Nods.)* She makes lots of things to give away. I—I think she will make me another one. But she always makes something for new babies. She would have made something for your baby if she had known.

Mahli's father: *(From off stage.)* Mahli!

Mahli: I'm coming. *(He starts to leave, then turns back.)* Anyway, maybe your baby will be a shepherd when he grows up. *(He hurries out and the stage darkens.)*

SS1868

CHRISTMAS SONGS
AND ACTIVITIES

Shining Star Publications, Copyright © 1988, A Division of Good Apple, Inc.

SS1868

LET'S MAKE IT A MUSICAL!
TIPS FOR USING CHRISTMAS SONGS ON STAGE

The objectives of elementary school music are based upon the experiences necessary to the development of the whole child. The range of learning runs from developing individual ability, to singing simple songs rhythmically, in tune and with light tone, to the singing of parts in the upper grades.

Singing develops vocal skills and good articulation. It promotes opportunities for frequent participation in programs. Also, through music, children develop an appreciation for, and understanding of, our cultural heritage.

Many of the fine traits of Christian character revealed in later life have their roots in the experiences of childhood. Worship is certainly one of these experiences.

This book has been planned to enrich the worship of children. All the music has been written within the range of children's voices. Tunes selected are joyous, attractive and singable.

Activity songs are provided to give a well balanced musical program. Encourage children to be creative in acting out songs. Use plenty of walking, clapping, marching and skipping.

The music included may be utilized in a variety of ways. Some may be used for solos, others for group singing, either in combination with plays and choral readings or as selections by the singing choir.

If you are planning to use the songs as part of your Christmas performance, here are some tips for preparation:

1. Sing all the songs with the children to find out which ones they enjoy singing the most. Let them help decide which ones they would like to perform.

2. Practice singing only for initial rehearsals. The entire cast should learn all the verses to all the songs that will be performed. Assign solo parts where you feel your cast members have the ability and where it is appropriate.

3. If accompaniment is not available at each rehearsal, practice with taped music. If musical instruments (example, bells) are to be part of the performance, have children practice with instruments after the first few rehearsals.

4. Decide where the songs will be used during the play and practice singing while rehearsing the play script. Children dressed as stars, lambs, angels can often be assigned solos to lengthen the play and thus include additional children.

5. Experiment by playing some of the songs softly in the background during narration. Would that add to the quality of your performance? Can songs be played softly before and after the performance to set the proper mood as audience is entering and leaving auditorium.

6. Copies of the songs can be reproduced if you want the audience to join in and sing some songs during or after the performance. How you can use the songs will depend on your performance. Be imaginative and let the children help make some of the decisions. Any way you choose to use the songs that follow, they will certainly help you make the holidays more merry. Remember this Christmas, "Make a joyful noise unto the Lord."

CHRISTMAS BELLS

Words and music by Helen Friesen

FOLLOW-UP ACTIVITIES

1. Have the children make bell decorations for their homes. Have available several patterns, glue, glitter, sequins and scissors. With a hole punch, punch a hole in the top of each bell and attach string or yarn for hanging bell.

2. The melody is actually on the bottom line with the bell-like accompaniment on top to be played softly. Use bells to ring and turn **CHRISTMAS BELLS** into an action song.

3. Name some happy sounds that only people can make. Example: laughter, whistling, singing, cheering, etc. Sing the song, replacing the ding, dong, ding, dong, Christmas bells are ringing, with ho, ho, ho, ho, Christmas laughter is ringing, or (whistle), (whistle), (whistle), Christmas cheer is ringing, etc. Let the children think up new words for the song using happy sounds that only people can make. Sing all the new versions for the song **CHRISTMAS BELLS**.

SS1868

BETHLEHEM!

Words and music by Grace Click

Our God looked down from Hea-ven on all the lit-tle
Now Beth-le-hem could nev-er boast of its size or
towns. He chose a tin-y vill-age from
fun. Yet it gained last-ing glor-y through
thou-sands all a- round. YES! Je-sus would be born... Where
God's be-lov-ed Son.
Dav-i'd lived and grew, and He would tell His people — In Mi-cah 5, Verse two.

FOLLOW-UP ACTIVITIES

1. Construct Bethlehem with empty boxes of various sizes (tissue boxes, cracker boxes, cake mix boxes, etc.) and cover them with construction, shelf or butcher paper of neutral colors. Then use crayons, chalk or charcoal in black, gray and brown tones to color "buildings." Let the children bring in anything they choose to create a miniature Bethlehem. Don't forget to include the stable.

2. Have the children make a Christmas Mosaic. Pass out the patterns found on pages 93, 94, 95 and 96. Children cut out and then trace around the shape of his/her choice. Mount pictures on light cardboard. Apply glue to areas to be filled in, one at a time. Fill in the pictures with uncooked rice dyed with different colors of food coloring.

SS1868

FOR UNTO US A CHILD IS BORN

Music by Helen Friesen
Text from Isaiah 9:6

FOLLOW-UP ACTIVITIES

Make musical instruments to accompany this lively tune.

Ring: Suspend different-sized pieces of metal, glass, pottery or wood. Hit with a mallet.

Drums: Stretch vinyl, tire inner tubing, a balloon, or rawhide across a coffee can, oatmeal box, coconut shell, box or garbage can. Hit with a mallet.

Flutes: Blow across bottle, glass jugs, plastic or metal tubes closed on one end. Use clay, cotton wads or glue to close tubing.

Scrape: Rub sandpaper, notched sticks, notebook spirals, air vents, tree bark, jawbones, a vegetable grater or anything textured.

Jingles: Affix flattened pop bottle caps, small bells, pieces of metal or hard plastic to a hoop, wristband, ankle strap or stick. Shake!

Stringed instruments: Stretch rubber bands, fishing wire or string across a cigar box, hunting bow, wishbone or plastic container. Pluck!

Rattles: Enclose rice, dried peas, shot, popcorn, beans, etc., in a jar, can, bottle, balloon or carton. Shake!

SS1868

BETHLEHEM EPHRATAH

Words and music by
Helen Friesen

Text taken from Micah 5:2 (KJV)

But thou, Beth-le-hem Eph-ra-tah, — though thou be lit-tle a-mong the thou-sands of Judah, yet out of thee shall He come forth un-to me that is to be rul-er in Is-ra-el; whose go--ings forth have been from of old, have been from of old, from ev-er-last-ing.

FOLLOW-UP ACTIVITIES

1. How does the music of this song make you feel? Discuss how music can put us in moods. Play the song faster, then slower, and see if the mood changes. Play familiar tunes at different tempos and see if the children recognize them.

2. Have the children make a Bethlehem mobile by cutting Christmas shapes from light cardboard. Decorate with markers, glitter, sequins and ribbon. Using a hole punch, punch holes where needed to connect mobile pieces with yarn. Hang mobiles and watch them flutter. (See patterns on pages 93-96.)

3. Have the children find the prophecy regarding Bethlehem as the birthplace of Jesus in the Old Testament. (Micah 5:2)

SS1868

HE CARES FOR YOU AND ME

Words by Helen Kitchell Evans

Music by Joe Anne Berkel

Melody Fast

FOLLOW-UP ACTIVITIES

1. Stained-glass windows are familiar features of churches. Encourage the children to make their own "stained-glass" Christmas pictures. Begin by having each child draw or trace a Christmas picture. (See patterns on pages 93, 94, 95 and 96). Then color the picture with crayons. Next rub the picture with cooking oil. This will make the picture translucent and allow light to pass through it. Cut out a frame for the picture using black construction paper. Glue or staple the frame to the picture. Hang pictures in a window so the light will shine through them.

2. The song speaks of His care for us. Have each child write a list, naming ways they know God cares for them.

Shining Star Publications, Copyright © 1988, A Division of Good Apple, Inc.

SS1868

HALLELUJAH

Words by Helen Kitchell Evans

Sung Lively

Music by Joe Anne Berkel

Hal-le- lu-jah, sing praise! Hal-le- lu-jah, sing praise!

Praise to our Sav-ior so dear___. Hal-le lu-jah, sing praise!

Hal-le- lu-jah, sing praise! The month of His birth-day is

here___! Hal- le- lu- jah!

BENEDICTION

Text based on Jude 1:21

Slowly

Music by Joe Anne Berkel

Keep your-selves in the love of God. A_____men.

FOLLOW-UP ACTIVITIES

1. Use these songs to open and close any Christmas performance that you are planning for the holiday season!

2. Rewrite the benediction. Ask children to think of a new line for the benediction. Explain that they will need to have an appropriate number of syllables in their new benediction. Sing everyone's new song.

LUKE'S STORY

Text from Luke 2:8-11

Music by Helen Friesen

FOLLOW-UP ACTIVITIES

While the song is being sung, have several children pantomime the actions of the song. Costumes and props could add to the fun!

SS1868

CHRISTMAS NIGHT

Words and music by Helen Friesen

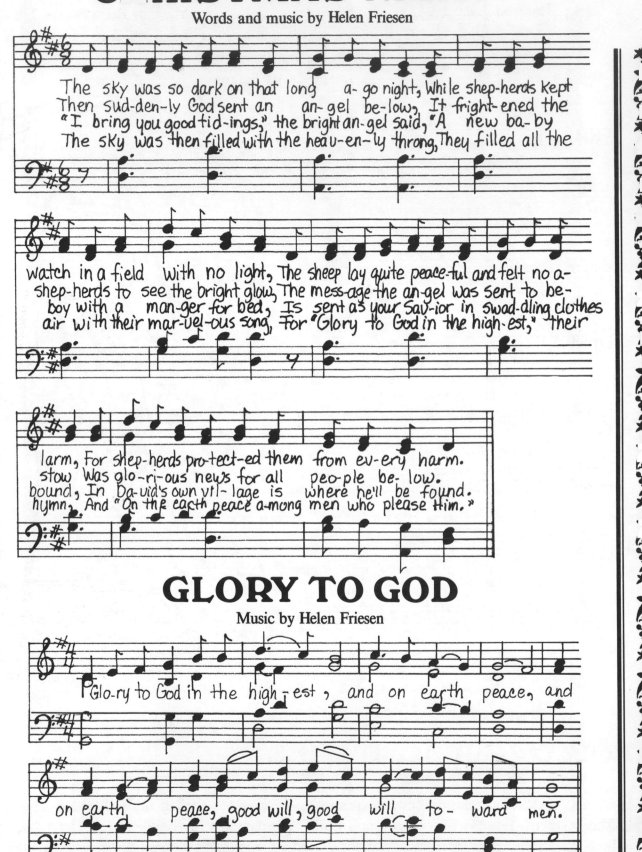

The sky was so dark on that long a-go night, While shep-herds kept
Then sud-den-ly God sent an an-gel be-low, It fright-ened the
"I bring you good tid-ings," the bright an-gel said, "A new ba-by
The sky was then filled with the heav-en-ly throng, They filled all the

watch in a field with no light, The sheep lay quite peace-ful and felt no a-
shep-herds to see the bright glow, The mess-age the an-gel was sent to be-
boy with a man-ger for bed, Is sent as your Sav-ior in swad-dling clothes
air with their mar-vel-ous song, For "Glo-ry to God in the high-est," their

larm, For shep-herds pro-tect-ed them from ev-ery harm.
stow Was glo-ri-ous news for all peo-ple be-low.
bound, In Da-vid's own vil-lage is where he'll be found.
hymn, And "On the earth peace a-mong men who please Him."

GLORY TO GOD

Music by Helen Friesen

Glo-ry to God in the high-est, and on earth peace, and

on earth peace, good will, good will to-ward men.

FOLLOW-UP ACTIVITIES

Angels paid many visits during this sacred moment in history. Send the children on a search through the four Gospels to record all the times when an angel paid a visit to the earth during the first Christmas season. Encourage children to list the person visited by an angel, the purpose of the visit and the Scripture verse(s) where the visit is described.

Shining Star Publications, Copyright © 1988, A Division of Good Apple, Inc.

SS1868

LITTLE SHEPHERD

Words by Dorthy Zimmerman
Music by Carver Sutton

Little Shepherd, on that night,

did you see that star so bright?

When you heard the angels' song,

did you try to sing a—long?

And did your eyes grow round with joy,

when you saw the ba-by boy?

Lit-tle Shepherd right from the start

did he stay forever in your heart?

FOLLOW-UP ACTIVITIES

Have the children pretend they are newspaper reporters living in Bethlehem at the time of the birth of Jesus. Encourage each child to interview a shepherd (children take turns telling the story to each other) and then write a newspaper story that gives all the facts found in the Christmas story from a shepherd's point of view.

SS1868

WHEN CHRIST WAS BORN

Words and music by Helen Friesen

FOLLOW-UP ACTIVITIES

1. Several weeks before Christmas begin a mural of the events leading up to the birth of Christ. Have the children study Luke, chapters 1 and 2. The class may decide where their mural is to begin: Mary's angelic visitation, the trek to Bethlehem, the inn, the stable. Plan the mural and assign (or ask for volunteers) different portions of the story to individuals or small groups. The mural could then be displayed in a church foyer or lobby. (See patterns on pages 93-96.)

2. Hold a class discussion on why the children think Jesus was born in a stable, not a palace. List the characteristics of a stable. Then arrange for the class to visit an actual stable, if possible. Conduct a creative writing activity where the children write modern-day stories about a child born in a stable. Share the stories.

SS1868

CHRISTMAS STARLIGHT

by Maurine Wagner

FOLLOW-UP ACTIVITIES

1. There must have been many star-filled nights on the road to Bethlehem. I wonder what Joseph and Mary dreamed about as they slept each night on their journey leading up to that "night of nights." Draw or paint a picture to illustrate one of Joseph or Mary's dreams.

2. Joseph was a very important man in the Scriptures. He was so important that one of the Gospel writers felt it was necessary to trace his lineage all the way back to Abraham. Look up the word "genealogy" in the dictionary. Then look up Joseph's genealogy in Matthew 1. Using a bulletin board, have the children make a family tree or chart showing the lineage of this great man, Joseph, all the way back to Abraham.

3. As a bonus activity, search through Genesis to discover the lineage of Abraham and extend Joseph's line on the family tree or chart all the way back to Adam!

SS1868

THE WISE MEN

Words and music by
Helen Friesen

1. From the East came wise men from a-far Searching for a King, led
2. Her-od told the wise men, "Go and look, Find that Ba-by fore-told
3. In a house the wise men found the child With His moth-er Mar-y

by a star, Quest-ioned Her-od 'bout the new-born King,
in the "Book," On to Beth-le- hem the wise men went
by His side. In a dream God warned them to take care

Herod shook be-cause he knew of no such thing.
For this spec-ial trip the star to them was sent.
Not with bad King Her-od their good news to share.

FOLLOW-UP ACTIVITIES

1. We aren't sure just exactly how far the wise men had to travel. But we know they must have had to travel a very long distance from somewhere. Have each child make a diorama using an old shoe box or other box of similar size to depict the wise men's journey. With box on its side, paint or draw the background on paper. Then glue it into place in the box. Remember to cover the bottom, top and sides of the inside of the box as it sits on its side. Make figures of wise men from pipe cleaners. Cover with scraps of cloth to represent clothing. Place these figures in diorama. Pipe cleaner camels or horses could also be used to complete the dioramas.

2. King Herod was a wicked man. Find out what he did that the wise men were forewarned about in their dream by reading the entire second chapter of Matthew.

SS1868

COSTUMES AND SCENERY
THE FINISHING TOUCHES!

On the following pages you will find suggestions and patterns for making simple costumes and scenery for Christmas performances. Remember to keep it simple. If costumes become too elaborate and the scenery and props too complicated, it will detract from the overall beauty of the Christmas story, which should never be lost. To keep costs down, use what you have on hand or ask for donations before you purchase anything. Use your imagination! The best source of ideas is right in your own head and the children's heads! Put your heads together, look around, and you'll be amazed at the great costume and scenery ideas you will develop. Getting ready for the performance should be as much fun as the big PRODUCTION.

Use an overhead projector to enlarge any of the patterns found on pages 93, 94, 95 and 96 for backdrops or stand-up scenery. Trace the patterns you want to enlarge on some clear transparency material and place it on your projector. Then make illustrations as large or as small as you desire. You can project the images directly onto cardboard, wood or whatever material you are using.

ROBES FOR MARY AND JOSEPH
Basic robe pattern for all

A twin-size sheet can be used to make a loose fitting costume. Use stripes and dark solid colors for Joseph and pastel colors for Mary. Fold sheet in half lengthwise. Fold again from top to bottom. Cut a pattern like the one shown. For children adjustments can be made for hem and arm length. Stitch the side seam and under the arm. Raw edges may be hemmed by turning up once. For more color, braid or fringe can be added at necklines or hems. Tie at waist with a cord or a man's necktie. Mary's headcovering can be a contrasting 36″ x 36″ piece of fabric. Center on head and hold in place with bobby pins or stretchy headband.

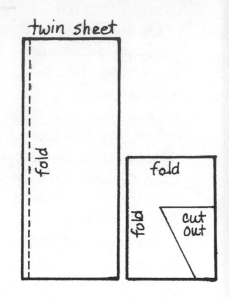

twin sheet

fold

fold

fold

cut out

20″

20″

20″

SHEPHERDS' COSTUMES

head measurement plus 12″

8″

10″

A shepherd's robe can be an old bathrobe or follow the directions for Joseph's robe found above. For the shepherd's headcovering, use an old white sheet. Cut a triangle with 20″ sides. Measure around forehead. Take a brightly colored piece of fabric (print or solid) that measures at least 12″ longer than head measurement. Make it about 8″ wide. Roll the fabric into a rope. Place the white, triangular cloth on top of shepherd's head with one point hanging down the back of his neck. Take the rolled fabric, tie around forehead to secure the white drape, and tuck in the tied ends.

To make a shepherd's staff you will need a broomstick or mop handle, a cardboard tubing from wrapping paper and 10″ cardboard, hook-shaped, for the crook of the staff. Staple or glue the hook-shaped piece to the gift-wrap tubing. Then attach the tubing to one end of the broomstick or mop handle with tape or glue. Paint the whole staff brown.

SS1868

DRESSING THE KINGS
Costumes for Herod and the wise men

Using the basic robe pattern described on page 90, a king's costume can be made for either King Herod or the three wise men. Fancier or more colorful fabric will suggest a more costly garment. Red, purple and royal blue are always very regal-looking colors to use for these costumes. Gold braid trim or pieces of old costume jewelry can be glued or sewn on the fabric.

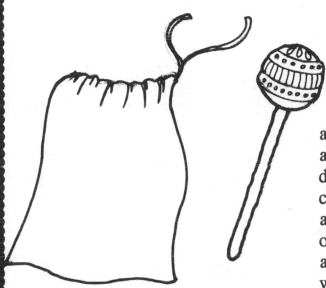

A simple cape can be added by sewing a 2″ hem at the end of a rectangular piece of fabric and running a heavy piece of yarn or cord through the end to draw up and tie around the neck of King Herod's costume. A jeweled scepter can be added to his regal appearance by gluing a Styrofoam ball to the end of a piece of dowling or the empty cylinder from a roll of gift wrap. The entire scepter can be covered with aluminum foil and decorated with sequins, pieces of old costume jewelry or even painted bottle caps.

To make crowns, simply cut various sizes of star-shapes from cardboard. Decorate them with glitter, paint, scraps of fancy material or trim. Fold a 2″ strip of construction paper in half to form a 1″ strip. Staple the decorated stars to the center portion of each headband and then fit a headband to the head of each king.

The gifts carried by the wise men can be made from shoe boxes, oatmeal boxes, fancy shaped bottles covered with aluminum foil or gold foil gift wrap. Decorate them by gluing on sequins, colored yarn twisted into a pattern or design, and pieces of old costume jewelry.

SS1868

CLOTHES FOR ANGELS

Make angel costumes from white sheets following basic robe pattern described on page 90. Gold tinsel tied around the waist and attached to the neckline will make angels glow. Gold ribbons may be tied around foreheads. Halos for angels can be made by bending heavy wire or old coat hangers into the desired shapes. The hoop at the top of the halo can be covered with tinsel garland.

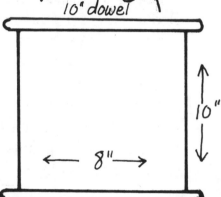

10" dowel

10"

← 8" →

NARRATOR FASHIONS

He or she should be dressed in costume. Narration may be read from a scroll. This can be made with two dowels and a paper bag. Cut strip of paper from bag 8″ wide and 10″-12″ long. Using two 10″ dowels, glue the end of the brown paper to each. Tape narrator's part on the paper and roll up. Secure with colored cord.

SANDAL CRAFT

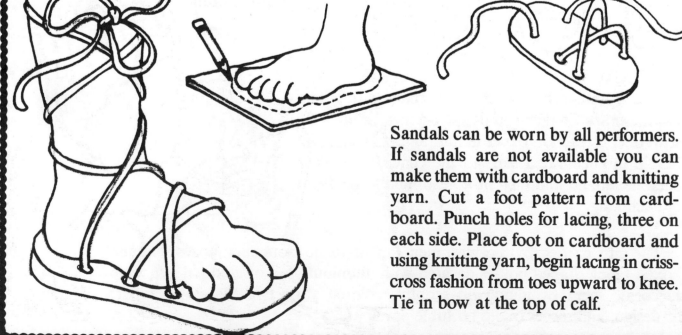

Sandals can be worn by all performers. If sandals are not available you can make them with cardboard and knitting yarn. Cut a foot pattern from cardboard. Punch holes for lacing, three on each side. Place foot on cardboard and using knitting yarn, begin lacing in crisscross fashion from toes upward to knee. Tie in bow at the top of calf.

SS1868

SCENERY PATTERNS

Flannel board cutouts
Bulletin board patterns
Clip 'n' copy Christmas graphics

The reproducible Christmas figures on this and the three pages that follow can be used in dozens of creative ways to make the Christmas season more joyful. Here are a few tips for using the Christmas graphics:

1. Use an overhead projector to enlarge for play scenery.
2. Reproduce on light cardboard. Cut out and attach flannel strips to the back of each figure for telling the stories found on pages 5-20.
3. Use an overhead projector to enlarge figures for bulletin boards.
4. Use as greeting card illustrations. Duplicate enough for each child on construction paper. Children can decorate cards with markers, crayons, paint and glitter. Use Scripture verses or phrases for card greetings.
5. Reduce to make patterns for Christmas stickers and awards. (Most print shops can reproduce copy to any size desired.)
6. Use an overhead projector to enlarge figures for a hall mural. Include all the figures in appropriate order to tell the Christmas story. Have children attach Bible verses in sequential order under pictures. Use colored chalk to make soft, pastel pictures.
7. Reproduce on light cardboard. Give each student a set of figures and yarn to create his/her own Christmas mobile. Punch holes in the top and bottom of figures and tie together in a balanced fashion.

Village Folk

Mary on Donkey

SS1868

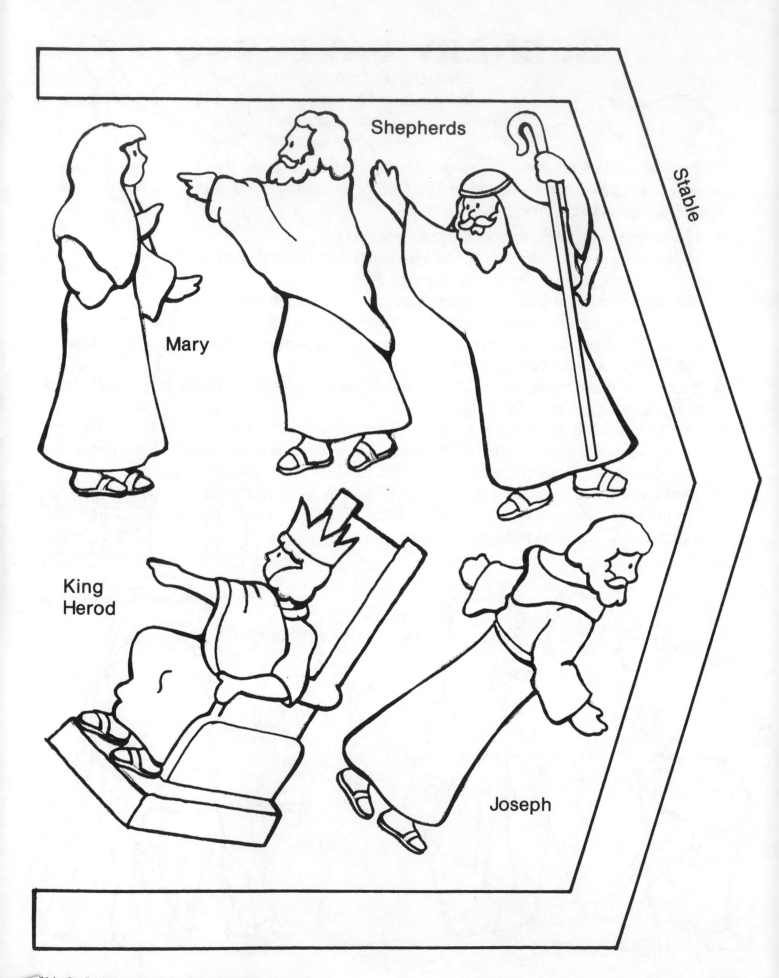

Shepherds

Stable

Mary

King
Herod

Joseph

SS1868

Angelic host

Doves

Gold

Gifts of Wise Men

Camel

Herald Angel

SS1868

Donkey

Three Wise Men

Baby
Jesus
in manger

Cattle/Oxen

Lamb/Sheep

Star

SS1868